THE HUMAN BODY
How It Works

The Circulatory System

THE HUMAN BODY
How It Works

THE HUMAN BODY
How It Works

The Circulatory System

Susan Whittemore

INTRODUCTION BY

Denton A. Cooley, M.D.
President and Surgeon-in-Chief
of the Texas Heart Institute
Clinical Professor of Surgery at the
University of Texas Medical School, Houston, Texas

CHELSEA HOUSE
PUBLISHERS
An imprint of Infobase Publishing

THE CIRCULATORY SYSTEM
Copyright © 2009 by Infobase Publishing

Chelsea House
An imprint of Infobase Publishing
132 West 31st Street
New York NY 10001

Library of Congress Cataloging-in-Publication Data

Whittemore, Susan.
  The circulatory system / Susan Whittemore.
    p. cm. -- (The human body: how it works)
  Includes bibliographical references and index.
  ISBN 978-1-60413-376-9 (hardcover)
  1. Cardiovascular system--Juvenile literature. 2. Blood--Circulation--Juvenile literature. I. Title. II. Series.

  QP103.W458 2008
  612.1--dc22

                                      2008042413

Chelsea House books are available at special discounts when purchased in bulk quantities for businesses, associations, institutions, or sales promotions. Please call our Special Sales Department in New York at (212) 967-8800 or (800) 322-8755.

You can find Chelsea House on the World Wide Web at
http://www.chelseahouse.com

Series design by Erika Arroyo, Erik Lindstrom
Cover design by Ben Peterson

Printed in the United States of America

Bang EJB 10 9 8 7 6 5 4 3 2 1

This book is printed on acid-free paper.

All links and Web addresses were checked and verified to be correct at the time of publication. Because of the dynamic nature of the Web, some addresses and links may have changed since publication and may no longer be valid.

Contents

Introduction

THE HUMAN BODY IS AN INCREDIBLY COMPLEX AND
amazing structure. At best, it is a source of strength, beauty,
and wonder. We can compare the healthy body to a well-
designed machine whose parts work smoothly together. We
can also compare it to a symphony orchestra in which each
instrument has a different part to play. When all of the musi-
cians play together, they produce beautiful music.

From a purely physical standpoint, our bodies are made
mainly of water. We are also made of many minerals, including calcium, phosphorous, potassium, sulfur, sodium, chlo-
rine, magnesium, and iron. In order of size, the elements of
the body are organized into cells, tissues, and organs. Related
organs are combined into systems, including the musculo-
skeletal, cardiovascular, nervous, respiratory, gastrointestinal,
endocrine, and reproductive systems.

Our cells and tissues are constantly wearing out and
being replaced without our even knowing it. In fact, much
of the time, we take the body for granted. When it is working properly, we tend to ignore it. Although the heart beats
about 100,000 times per day and we breathe more than 10
million times per year, we do not normally think about these
things. When something goes wrong, however, our bodies
tell us through pain and other symptoms. In fact, pain is a
very effective alarm system that lets us know the body needs
attention. If the pain does not go away, we may need to see a
doctor. Even without medical help, the body has an amazing
ability to heal itself. If we cut ourselves, the blood-clotting
system works to seal the cut right away, and the immune

defense system sends out special blood cells that are programmed to heal the area.

During the past 50 years, doctors have gained the ability to repair or replace almost every part of the body. In my own field of cardiovascular surgery, we are able to open the heart and repair its valves, arteries, chambers, and connections. In many cases, these repairs can be done through a tiny "keyhole" incision that speeds up patient recovery and leaves hardly any scar. If the entire heart is diseased, we can replace it altogether, either with a donor heart or with a mechanical device. In the future, the use of mechanical hearts will probably be common in patients who would otherwise die of heart disease.

Until the mid-twentieth century, infections and contagious diseases related to viruses and bacteria were the most common causes of death. Even a simple scratch could become infected and lead to death from "blood poisoning." After penicillin and other antibiotics became available in the 1930s and 1940s, doctors were able to treat blood poisoning, tuberculosis, pneumonia, and many other bacterial diseases. Also, the introduction of modern vaccines allowed us to prevent childhood illnesses, smallpox, polio, flu, and other contagions that used to kill or cripple thousands.

Today, plagues such as the "Spanish flu" epidemic of 1918–19, which killed 20 to 40 million people worldwide, are unknown except in history books. Now that these diseases can be avoided, people are living long enough to have long-term (chronic) conditions such as cancer, heart failure, diabetes, and arthritis. Because chronic diseases tend to involve many organ systems or even the whole body, they cannot always be cured with surgery. These days, researchers are doing a lot of work at the cellular level, trying to find the underlying causes of chronic illnesses. Scientists recently finished mapping the human genome, which is a set of coded "instructions" programmed into our cells. Each cell contains 3 billion "letters" of this code. By showing how the body is made, the human genome will help researchers prevent and treat disease at its source, within the cells themselves.

The body's long-term health depends on many factors, called risk factors. Some risk factors, including our age, sex, and family history of certain diseases, are beyond our control. Other important risk factors include our lifestyle, behavior, and environment. Our modern lifestyle offers many advantages but is not always good for our bodies. In western Europe and the United States, we tend to be stressed, overweight, and out of shape. Many of us have unhealthy habits such as smoking cigarettes, abusing alcohol, or using drugs. Our air, water, and food often contain hazardous chemicals and industrial waste products. Fortunately, we can do something about most of these risk factors. At any age, the most important things we can do for our bodies are to eat right, exercise regularly, get enough sleep, and refuse to smoke, overuse alcohol, or use addictive drugs. We can also help clean up our environment. These simple steps will lower our chances of getting cancer, heart disease, or other serious disorders.

These days, thanks to the Internet and other forms of media coverage, people are more aware of health-related matters. The average person knows more about the human body than ever before. Patients want to understand their medical conditions and treatment options. They want to play a more active role, along with their doctors, in making medical decisions and in taking care of their own health.

I encourage you to learn as much as you can about your body and to treat your body well. These things may not seem too important to you now, while you are young, but the habits and behaviors that you practice today will affect your physical well-being for the rest of your life. The present book series, The Human Body: How It Works, is an excellent introduction to human biology and anatomy. I hope that it will awaken within you a lifelong interest in these subjects.

Denton A. Cooley, M.D.
President and Surgeon-in-Chief
of the Texas Heart Institute
Clinical Professor of Surgery at the
University of Texas Medical School, Houston, Texas

1

Human Heart Transplants

IN 1967, DR. CHRISTIAN BARNARD, A SURGEON IN SOUTH AFRICA, performed the first human heart transplant. He transplanted the heart of a young woman who was brain-dead as a result of an auto accident into a 53-year-old male grocery store owner who suffered from heart disease. The surgery was a success, although the patient died 18 days later from pneumonia, most likely a result of the immune-suppressing drugs given to him to prevent rejection of the heart. Dr. Barnard's success fueled a flurry of heart transplant surgeries in the next year, but the survival rate was so low that, by 1970, only 18 transplants had been performed.

Since then, more than 60,000 transplants have been performed in the United States alone, with more than 2,000 Americans receiving life-saving heart transplants every year. Although the survival rate of transplant patients has improved significantly from those earlier days, 25% of heart transplant recipients still die within 5 years. However, other recipients are more fortunate. Tony Huesman, for example, has lived for 30 years with his transplanted heart. When he was 18, a bout with pneumonia severely weakened his heart muscle. His heart enlarged to four times its original size as a result of trying to pump **blood** in this weakened state.

While the surgical techniques used to perform heart transplants have not changed all that much, the development of better immune-supressing drugs has decreased rejections and improved the survival rates. However, there still are not enough hearts to go around—every year in the United States, hundreds of patients die waiting for a heart to become available. But technology may be coming to the rescue with a device called the HeartMate II (Figure 1.1). About the size of a D-cell battery, the device is implanted into the chest of an individual who is in severe heart failure. It assists the weakened heart in pumping blood through the body while the patient waits for a donor heart. An external battery pack keeps it running. The HeartMate II's small size means that it can be used in patients of all sizes. Other types of artificial hearts are so large that they cannot be used in small adults and children. What is even more amazing is that, in some patients, use of the HeartMate II has allowed the heart to recover and improve its function, enough so that they may not require a transplant after all.

Other scientists are trying to address the problem of donor heart shortages by creating nonmechanical, living replacement hearts. Pigs that have human-size hearts have been genetically engineered so that their tissues do not trigger an immune response and rejection when the hearts are transplanted into humans. These genetically engineered pigs lack a key enzyme, and this, at least in theory, allows for a pig-to-human transplant, a process known as *xenotransplantation*.

University of Minnesota researchers have developed the first "bioartifical heart" by taking a whole heart and stripping it of all its cells—a process called *decellularization*—so that just a scaffold of extracellular matrix remains. This architectural scaffold of a heart is then seeded with the patient's own stem cells, which mature into beating heart cells. (The heart scaffolds could be created from pigs or humans.) A heart generated through the use of this technique would be a perfect tissue match to the recipient and therefore would not trigger rejection. Experiments using rodent and pig hearts have been very promising, and the technique could be adapted for the development of other organs like the kidney, pancreas, and liver.

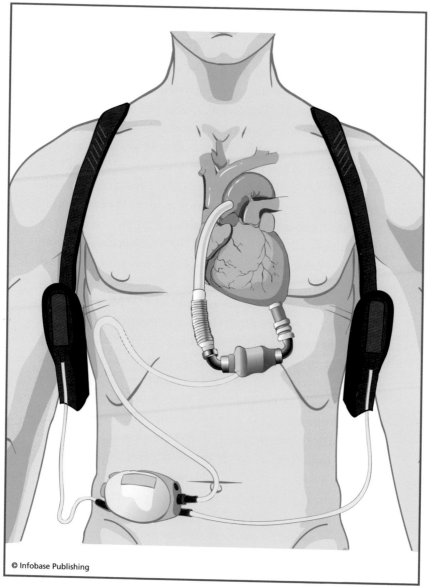

© Infobase Publishing

Figure 1.1   The HeartMate II helps a failing heart to pump blood. It has been used in patients waiting for a heart transplant as well to assist hearts in which the left ventricle cannot pump adequate amounts of blood. It is powered by a small, external battery pack.

The progress made in techniques for heart transplants is important because human life is impossible without a functioning heart. The heart pumps blood and all the important substances it carries to and from the tissues through the **circulatory system**. Humans also need a healthy, strong heart to lead an active and full life. Today, heart disease remains the leading cause of death in the United States, so many researchers are investigating how individuals can prevent heart disease in the first place, thus avoiding the need for transplants.

The remaining chapters of this book examine the structure and function of different aspects of the human circulatory system. Chapter 2 provides an overview of the circulatory system. Chapter 3 describes the composition of blood, its role in transporting various subtances, and the different types of cells it contains. Chapter 4 is focused on hemoglobin, the molecule in red blood cells that transports oxygen. The anatomy of the heart is addressed in Chapter 5, while Chapter 6 describes the cardiac cycle and how the heart works. Chapter 7 addresses the different types of blood vessels and traces the path of one red blood cell through the circulatory system. The control of blood pressure and the distribution of blood flow to various organs is described in Chapter 8, which also looks at how the circulatory system responds to the challenges of exercise and hemorrhage.

2

Overview of the Human Circulatory System

HAVE YOU EVER WONDERED HOW THE CELLS IN YOUR LITTLE toe get the nutrients and oxygen they need? Every cell in the human body needs oxygen and nutrients and, at the same time, must be able to rid itself of waste products that can become toxic if allowed to build up. In the lungs, oxygen from inhaled air is absorbed into the blood, while in the small intestine, nutrients from food enter the blood. Both oxygen and nutrients must be distributed to all cells in the body, including those in your little toe. The human circulatory system consists of the heart, blood, and a closed system of vessels that includes the **arteries**, **veins**, and **capillaries**. This system carries oxygen and nutrients to all the body cells and picks up waste products for degradation and disposal by the liver, kidneys, and lungs. It is easy to understand why all the other body systems depend on a healthy, functioning circulatory system.

Diffusion is the process in which molecules move from a region of higher concentration to a region of lower concentration. Diffusion is not fast enough to support the oxygen and nutrient demands of a large multicellular organism like a human. Diffusion only works over very short distances. While humans do rely on diffusion between the blood and the air in the lungs, and between the blood and the cells in the capillaries, the delivery of blood to these sites of exchange must take place very rapidly and efficiently. Therefore, blood is transported throughout the human body by the process of **bulk flow**. In this process, blood is moved from regions of higher pressure to regions of lower pressure by the actions of the heart, the pump that pressurizes the blood to drive its flow. Such a system allows for the rapid transport of blood over long distances so it can deliver nutrients to, and carry away wastes from, all of the body's cells.

In humans, the heart and its delivery system have two separate circuits. The **pulmonary circuit**, supplied by the right side of the heart, receives blood returning to the heart from the body and pumps it to the lungs for reoxygenation and unloading of carbon dioxide (Figure 2.1). The **systemic circuit**, supplied by the left side of the heart, delivers the oxygenated blood to the entire body. In both circuits, the blood is pressurized in the heart and then travels through a series of blood vessels to the capillaries for exchange of materials with the cells. It is then returned to the heart.

The circulatory system is composed of different tissues. The four basic types of tissues in the body are: *epithelial*, *muscular*, *nervous*, and *connective*. All of them are found in the circulatory system. Epithelial tissue, such as the outer layers of the skin and the innermost layer of the digestive system, provides barriers between such organs and their environment, in addition to performing other important functions. In the circulatory system, the heart and blood vessels are lined with epithelial cells. Nervous tissue is involved in sensing and responding to our internal and external environments and supports communication and coordination among different organ systems. Nerves from the brain stem control important **cardiovascular** functions such as **heart rate** and **blood pressure**. Muscle tissue is involved in movement of the body, the movement of food through the digestive system, and, of course, the pumping of blood. Connective tissue represents a

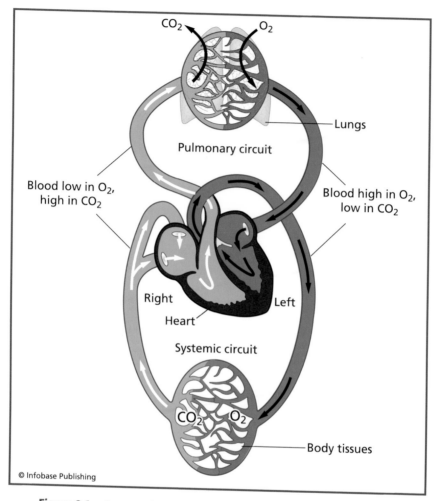

Figure 2.1 An overview of the human circulatory system. The system consists of two separate circuits: the pulmonary circuit, which carries deoxygenated blood to the lungs for oxygenation, and the systemic circuit, which supplies the entire body with oxygenated blood. The blood is shown in blue where it has reduced oxygen content and red when fully oxygenated. Note that in both circuits, arteries carry blood away from the heart, while veins carry blood returning to the heart.

very diverse group of tissues, including the bones and cartilage of the skeletal system, the collagen layer of the skin, fat tissue surrounding organs, and the blood.

CONNECTIONS

The human circulatory system is designed to rapidly and effi-ciently transport blood to all regions of the body. Blood is con-tained under pressure within a vascular system composed of several types of blood vessels. The human circulatory system is composed of two separate circuits: the pulmonary circuit, which carries blood to the lungs to be oxygenated, and the systemic circuit, which supplies the entire body with oxygen-ated blood.

Blood carries oxygen and nutrients needed by the body's respiring tissues. Blood also transports cellular wastes to elimination sites. Many of the other important functions of blood and the human circulatory system are addressed in the next chapter. Although diffusion drives the exchange of gases and molecules in the capillaries, blood must remain in rapid motion to perform its diverse functions. The heart serves as a pump, generating the blood pressures needed to achieve bulk flow of this fluid. The four-chambered heart of humans con-sists of two pumps that beat as one. The right side of the heart provides the pressure to propel blood through the pulmonary circuit, while the left side of the heart pumps blood through the systemic circuit.

3

The Composition of Blood

Blood can convey a lot of information about a person. For example, like other cells, white blood cells contain DNA which determines a person's unique genetic profile. Blood may also contain so-called "markers" that signal the presence of certain diseases, such as cancer, or indicate chemical imbalances, such as an iron deficiency. An individual's risk of suffering heart disease or level of exposure to a toxic substance can be determined from a blood sample. Blood levels of alcohol or other drugs can indicate a person's degree of impairment for performing certain tasks, such as driving. No other bodily tissue can provide such a range of information about a person's health.

BLOOD IS A FLUID TISSUE

Blood is a fluid tissue. It is classified as a connective tissue because it consists of cells surrounded by a fluid known as the **plasma**. Although many other connective tissues play important structural and protective roles, blood functions to distribute a wide variety of substances that are critical to life. Blood transports nutrients from their site of absorption in the digestive tract to the cells that require these nutrients.

Blood carries the waste products of the cells' activities to the lungs, liver, and kidneys for disposal from the body. It distributes hormones to organs to coordinate physiological functions. Red blood cells transport oxygen from the lungs to the cells, while white blood cells are important in fighting infection. Blood carries **clotting factors** and **platelets** to help prevent the blood loss that often occurs with injury. It also carries heat generated in the body core to other parts of the body, and distributes water and electrolytes to all of the tissues.

THE CELLS OF THE BLOOD

If we take a sample of whole blood and spin it down in a centrifuge to separate its major components, we would obtain a sample similar to the one shown in Figure 3.1. At the top of the centrifuged blood sample is the fluid portion, the plasma, which represents about 55% of the total volume. Beneath that is a whitish layer called the *buffy coat*. This layer contains **white blood cells**, or **leukocytes**, which fight diseases, and platelets, which function in blood clotting and the slowing of blood loss. This layer constitutes less than 1% of the total volume of blood. The remaining nearly 45% of blood consists of **red blood cells**, or **erythrocytes**, which carry oxygen to the tissues. The buffy coat and erythrocytes are the blood's solid components.

Red Blood Cells

Mature red blood cells are unusual because they are so structurally simple. In the bone marrow, immature red blood cells contain all the organelles that typical cells contain. But during their maturation process, before they enter the circulatory system, red blood cells lose many of their major organelles. A mature red blood cell does not have a nucleus and, therefore, has no means of activating genes or producing gene products. It has no ribosomes, mitochondria, or many of the other organelles that typical animal cells have. Each red

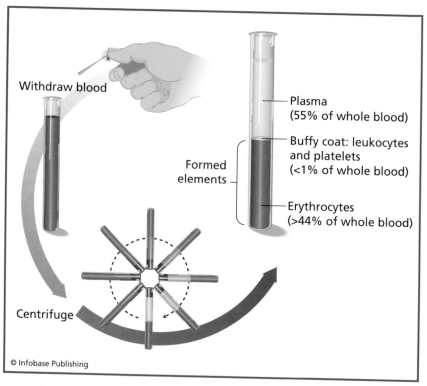

Withdraw blood

Plasma
(55% of whole blood)

Buffy coat: leukocytes
and platelets
(<1% of whole blood)

Formed
elements

Erythrocytes
(>44% of whole blood)

Centrifuge

© Infobase Publishing

Figure 3.1   When a sample of whole blood is spun in a centrifuge, the solid components settle to the bottom of the tube. Red blood cells (erythrocytes) constitute about 45% of the volume of blood. The white blood cells (leukocytes) and platelets represent less than 1% of the volume and are present in the buffy coat, a thin layer on top of the red blood cells. The remaining 55% of the volume is plasma, the liquid matrix surrounding the blood cells.

blood cell is a package of hemoglobin molecules. **Hemoglobin** is the red, iron-containing pigment that carries oxygen in the blood. The biconcave (concave on both sides) shape of the red blood cell allows it to fold and squeeze through small capillaries and provides a large surface area for oxygen diffusion. The structure and functions of hemoglobin will be addressed in more detail in Chapter 4.

Red Blood Cell Production

Because red blood cells cannot undergo cellular reproduction or repair, they typically survive for only 120 days. When a red blood cell starts to wear out, it is removed from circulation by the spleen. As a result, every day the human body must generate 250 billion replacement cells from the bone marrow.

The process of blood-cell formation is called **hematopoiesis**, and it occurs in bone marrow. **Hematopoietic stem cells** are *undifferentiated* cells—cells that can become a variety of blood-cell types depending on the signals they receive during their maturation process. They are found in the bone marrow. When stimulated to divide by certain growth factors, these stem cells generate two daughter cells. One of the daughter cells serves as a replacement stem cell for the parent cell and remains in the bone marrow. The other daughter cell *differentiates*, becomes committed to a certain developmental pathway, and matures into a specific type of blood cell.

As seen in Figure 3.2, once a hematopoietic stem cell differentiates into a *myeloblast*, this stem cell can give rise to many types of blood cells: granulocytes, monocytes (which become macrophages), **eosinophils**, **megakaryocytes** (which form platelets), and red blood cells. We can also see that lymphoblasts give rise to B and T cells, also known as **lymphocytes**.

The specific type of blood cell produced from hematopoietic stem cells depends on the growth factors present. For example, red blood-cell production is stimulated by the hormone **erythropoietin**. This hormone is synthesized by the kidneys and travels via the bloodstream to the bone marrow, where it binds to hormone receptors and promotes the production of mature red blood cells. If you travel to a high altitude where atmospheric oxygen levels are low, your kidneys will produce more erythropoietin to stimulate red blood-cell production and increase the oxygen-carrying capacity of the blood. The volume of whole blood occupied by red blood

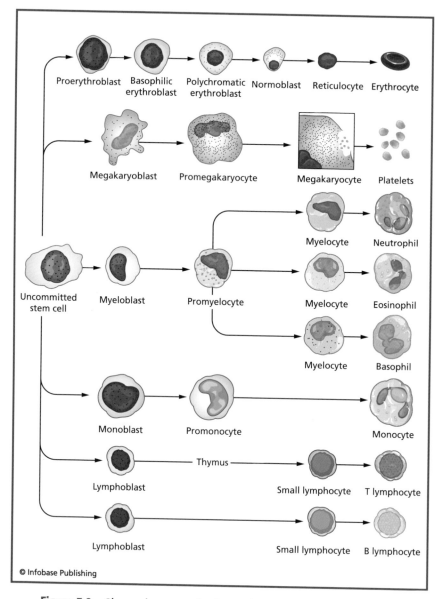

Proerythroblast Basophilic erythroblast Polychromatic erythroblast Normoblast Reticulocyte Erythrocyte

Megakaryoblast Promegakaryocyte Megakaryocyte Platelets

Myelocyte Neutrophil

Uncommitted stem cell Myeloblast Promyelocyte Myelocyte Eosinophil

Myelocyte Basophil

Monoblast Promonocyte Monocyte

Lymphoblast Thymus Small lymphocyte T lymphocyte

Lymphoblast Small lymphocyte B lymphocyte

Figure 3.2 Shown here are the formed elements of the blood. All blood cells arise from uncommitted stem cells located in the bone marrow. Note that during development, red blood cells lose many of their internal organelles. Mature red blood cells are biconcave and packed with hemoglobin. Platelets are cell fragments that are formed from megakaryocytes.

cells is called the **hematocrit** and is typically about 45%. The hematocrit of males is higher than that of females because the male sex steroid, testosterone, stimulates erythropoietin synthesis by the kidney.

ABO Blood Type and the Rh Factor

There are four different ABO blood types in the general human population: A, B, AB, and O. These designations refer to whether an individual possesses specific proteins with or without certain polysaccharides, also known as **antigens**, on the surface of their red blood cells. Individuals with type A blood have the A version of this antigen on the surface of their red blood cells, while type B individuals have the B version. Both the A and B antigens are present on the red blood cells of a person with type AB blood. Type O refers to the absence of both the A and B antigens (Figure 3.3).

If you know your blood type, you are aware that a person can be type A positive or type A negative. The "positive" and "negative" descriptors refer to the Rh, or "Rhesus," factor, which represents a different type of antigen that is also located on the surface of the red blood cell. A person with Rh positive blood has the Rh antigen, while a person with Rh negative blood does not have the Rh antigen. So, an individual with A positive blood has both the A antigen and the Rh antigen on the surface of their red blood cells. In contrast, A, B, and Rh antigens are absent from the red blood cells of a person with type O negative blood.

An individual with type A blood produces antibodies against the B antigen. **Antibodies** are produced by the B cells of the immune system to fight foreign invaders like viruses and bacteria. Antibodies help destroy these invaders by binding to the foreign antigens and triggering a series of events to destroy the antigen-bearing invader. To a person with type A blood, type B blood is perceived as a foreign and potentially harmful invader. Antibodies will bind to the B antigen and initiate

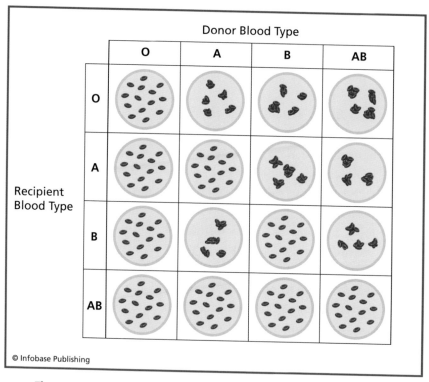

Figure 3.3 ABO blood type is determined by the presence or absence of the A and B antigens on the surface of the red blood cells. Blood type also determines which antibodies are present in the blood. The diagram shows which blood types are compatible. For example, when type A blood is given to a recipient with type B blood, the blood cells clump together, demonstrating their incompatibility.

events that lead to destruction of the type B blood cells. As with ABO blood type, an individual who has Rh negative blood (that is, has no Rh antigens on the surface of their red blood cells) will possess antibodies against the Rh factor.

Giving a person with type A blood a transfusion of type B blood can cause a *transfusion reaction* in which the transfused red blood cells are attacked by the recipient's antibodies. As a result, the transfused cells clump together and burst. The clumps may clog small blood vessels and interrupt blood flow, while the bursting of cells renders them useless for the transport of oxygen. Furthermore, the released hemoglobin can interfere with kidney function, likely causing kidney failure and possibly death. It is obviously important to use only compatible blood types in transfusions. Scientists are currently working to develop an artificial blood substitute that would avoid the problems associated with the collection, storage, and transfusion of human blood.

Figure 3.3 shows which donor blood types are compatible with the recipient's blood type. By examining the list of acceptable donor blood types, it is easy to understand why type O negative blood is in such high demand and why it is called the **universal donor blood type**. There are no A, B, or Rh antigens to trigger an immune reaction. Type AB positive blood is considered to be the **universal recipient blood type** in that an individual with type AB positive blood can safely receive transfusions of all other blood types.

WHITE BLOOD CELLS

Leukocytes, or white blood cells, help the body to defend itself against infection. Leukocytes are divided into two major groups: *granulocytes*, which have many granules, and *agranulocytes*, which have no granules. These cells are classified based on their staining patterns, which can be seen under a microscope.

Stained cells that show a multilobed nucleus and many stained granules are called **polymorphonuclear granulocytes**. There are three types of granulocytes (refer again to Figure 3.2). **Neutrophils** are the most abundant type and play a significant role in the inflammatory process. Eosinophils fight against multicellular parasites and are involved in allergic reactions. **Basophils** contribute to the inflammatory process by releasing the chemical histamine.

There are two types of agranulocytes: lymphocytes and monocytes. Lymphocytes possess little cytoplasm around their large nuclei and are key to specific immunity, the ability of the human immune system to target specific disease-causing agents. **Monocytes**, large cells with oval nuclei and only a few granules, represent another class of leukocytes. Upon entering tissues, these cells transform into macrophages, which can consume foreign cells or cellular debris and play a critical role in the destruction of infectious microorganisms.

Like red blood cells, all of these types of leukocytes are produced in the bone marrow, although some mature in organs such as the thymus gland.

PLATELETS

Platelets are small cell fragments that circulate in the blood in high numbers and promote clotting to reduce blood loss when blood vessels are damaged. Large cells in the bone marrow called megakaryocytes provide a constant source of these valuable cell fragments.

Platelets function in two key steps in the body's rapid response to stop bleeding. First, they form a plug at the wound site by sticking to the exposed collagen layer of the blood vessel (Figure 3.4). Once a few platelets bind, they become activated and release a variety of important chemicals. Some of the chemicals stimulate more platelets to bind to the site so that a platelet plug is formed. Other chemicals stimulate the damaged vessel to contract, decreasing the flow of blood to the site of injury, thus slowing blood loss.

In addition to their role in rapidly forming a plug, platelets are also involved in the next phase of preventing blood loss, which is called the **coagulation**, or blood-clotting, process. A blood clot forms around the platelet plug and helps to stabilize it. The plasma, which is the liquid portion of the blood, contains clotting factors (inactive forms of clotting enzymes). When certain clotting factors come into contact with the damaged area of the blood vessel, they are activated and trigger a cascade of events that leads to clot formation.

One of the key reactions involved in the clot formation cascade is the conversion of **prothrombin** to **thrombin**.

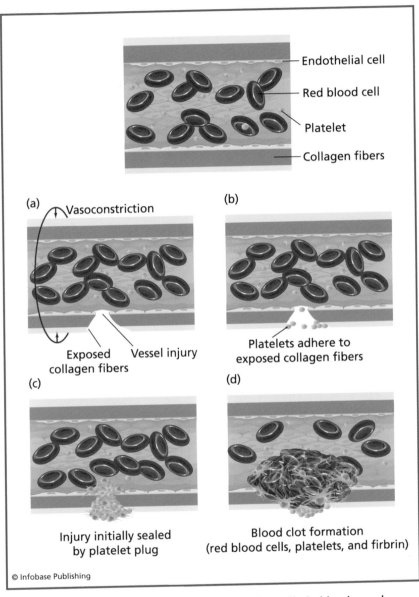

Endothelial cell

Red blood cell

Platelet

Collagen fibers

(a)

Vasoconstriction

(b)

Exposed
collagen fibers   Vessel injury

Platelets adhere to
exposed collagen fibers

(c)

(d)

Injury initially sealed
by platelet plug

Blood clot formation
(red blood cells, platelets, and firbrin)

Figure 3.4   Clot formation at a break in the wall of a blood vessel. Vasoconstriction reduces blood flow and blood loss. Platelets adhere to the damaged tissue, releasing chemoattractants that bring more platelets to the site. The plug formed as a result provides a temporary seal, allowing time for the blood vessel to repair the damage. The coagulation process generates the production of fibrin, which forms a meshlike tangle that traps red blood cells.

Thrombin is the plasma enzyme that activates the formation of a meshlike tangle of strands made of the protein **fibrin**. The fibrin strands form the structural scaffolding for the clot. Other plasma enzymes strengthen the fibrin network, which, once stabilized, begins to trap blood cells to complete the clot-formation process.

Unfortunately, damage to the blood vessels can result from factors other than injury. **Atherosclerosis** is a condition in which fatty deposits, or **plaque**, form on walls of arteries. This can cause damage to blood vessel walls. Exposure of the underlying vessel layers can trigger the clotting cascade, generating a blood clot that may block the vessel. If this clot formation occurs in a coronary artery, it may block blood

ARTIFICIAL BLOOD

Every year in the United States, more than 5 million people receive blood transfusions. Worldwide, more than 100 million units (45 million liters) of blood are needed for transfusions. While many people donate blood to replenish the ever-dwindling supplies in blood banks, experts state that there are not enough blood donations to meet demands. Furthermore, the collection and storage of blood is costly, and the blood has a limited shelf life. Blood must also be typed for the ABO and Rh antigens and screened for pathogens, such as HIV and hepatitis C, before it can be used. For these reasons, scientists have been working to develop a blood substitute, but reaching this goal has been harder than anticipated.

One of the more promising solutions involves the development of artificial hemoglobin, the oxygen transport molecule contained within red blood cells. A cell-free hemoglobin transfusion solution would avoid the need for blood typing and screening and would simplify storage requirements. Scientists have been trying to develop an artificial hemoglobin that functions like natural hemoglobin, but will work outside the specialized environment normally provided by the red blood cell. This hemoglobin solution presents flow, and hence oxygen flow, to the heart and cause a heart attack, a condition discussed in Chapter 5.

Many Americans have atherosclerosis, or "hardening of the arteries." Anticlotting drugs are frequently prescribed for this condition to reduce the risk of heart attack. One of the most commonly used drugs, aspirin, interferes with platelet aggregation, one of the early and key steps in triggering clot formation. Other anticlotting medications interfere with vitamin K production, a factor needed by the liver for the synthesis of clotting proteins. Certain drugs, called clot-busters, are used only after surgery or stroke to dissolve clots that have already formed. Clot-busters reduce the risk of strokes, also known as a cerebrovascular accidents (CVAs), which are

some important challenges, however. Unprotected hemoglobin is rapidly destroyed and transfusions of hemoglobin would need to be given repeatedly. In addition, free hemoglobin appears to trigger high blood pressure in some patients by stimulating constriction of the blood vessels; it can also cause kidney failure by blocking the kidney tubules. A recent development using chemically modified bovine (cow) hemoglobin, which has a much longer shelf life, appears to avoid some of the problems of using cell-free hemoglobin solutions as blood substitutes.

Another interesting approach involves the masking of the ABO and Rh antigens on the red blood cells by coating them with a polymer, essentially converting all blood types into type O negative, the universal blood donor type. In addition, a cell- and hemoglobin-free solution containing perfluorocarbons is currently being tested in clinical trials. Perfluorocarbons carry five times more oxygen than hemoglobin. The solutions containing these molecules can be sterilized and do not appear to trigger immune reactions. Hemoglobin substitutes, antigen-masking, and perfluorocarbon solutions represent just some of the blood-replacement possibilities under current investigation.

most commonly due to the blockage of a blood vessel in the brain by dislodged blood clots. If left untreated, the lack of oxygen to the area of the brain supplied by that blood vessel could result in the loss of whatever functions it controls.

Although some people develop blood clots that cause stroke and heart attack, other people suffer from an inability to form blood clots. **Hemophilia** refers to several hereditary blood-clotting disorders involving a deficiency in one or more of the clotting factors. The coagulation process involves a cascade of reactions and several clotting factors. Because each clotting factor initiates the next reaction in the cascade, a deficiency in any one of these factors can reduce the amount of thrombin and fibrin produced.

The most common type of hemophilia, known as hemophilia A, involves a deficiency in a clotting factor called factor VIII. One in 5,000 males in the United States has this disorder, and it affected many of the male descendants of Queen Victoria of England. The defective gene is carried on the X chromosome and is, therefore, sex-linked. Recombinant DNA technology has led to large-scale production of the factor VIII protein, which now helps to prevent the debilitating symptoms and death associated with the more severe cases of hemophilia A. Clotting factors that treat patients with other types of hemophilia are also now available through advances in this technology.

PLASMA

Plasma is the liquid, or extracellular (because of how it surrounds the blood cells) portion, of blood tissue. As discussed in the previous section, plasma contains proteins that are critical to the clotting process. In fact, to obtain plasma with its dissolved clotting proteins, it is necessary to include an anticoagulant, such as heparin, in the collection tube. If no anticoagulant is present in the tube, the blood will clot, removing clotting proteins such as fibrinogen in the process. Plasma without its clotting proteins is called **serum**.

Plasma contains a variety of other dissolved substances in addition to clotting proteins. **Albumins** and **globulins** are two additional classes of plasma proteins that serve a variety of important functions in the blood. For example, they help to maintain blood volume. The lack of these blood proteins in *kwashiorkor*, a type of severe malnutrition, causes abdominal bloating due to disruption in fluid balance. Albumin and globulin are involved in the transport of other substances, particularly hydrophobic molecules such as steroid hormones that do not dissolve well in plasma. Some of the globulins represent antibodies, proteins that are required for immunity against disease.

A variety of hormones can be detected in the plasma either directly dissolved in the fluid or bound to transport proteins. A plasma or serum sample can also provide levels of key electrolytes, gases, and nutrients. In Chapter 5, you will learn how blood and its precious cargo, oxygen, are circulated throughout the body.

CONNECTIONS

Blood is a connective tissue consisting of cells and cell fragments suspended in an extracellular fluid called plasma. Red blood cells constitute about 45% of the volume of whole blood. Their biconcave shape provides a large surface area for oxygen diffusion. These cells are packed with hemoglobin, the respiratory protein that binds and transports oxygen to the respiring tissues. White blood cells fight infection, and

(continues on page 32)

(continued from page 31)

platelets function in blood clotting. All blood cells originate from stem cells in the bone marrow.

Blood transports many important substances throughout the body. It transports oxygen from the lungs and nutrients from the digestive system to the tissues. Hormones are chemical messengers that are transported to their target tissues by the blood. Blood also carries cellular waste products for elimination. It distributes heat, water, and electrolytes throughout the body. It is no wonder that we are often asked by physicians to provide a blood sample. No other bodily tissue can provide such a diversity of information about our health.

4

Oxygen Transport:
The Role of Hemoglobin

IN THE LAST CHAPTER, YOU LEARNED THAT RED BLOOD CELLS are stripped-down cells packed with the respiratory protein hemoglobin. This chapter will focus on the structure and function of this important transport protein. Hemoglobin and a related protein called myoglobin bind oxygen and were the first proteins to be intensively studied by biochemists. As a result, the relationship between their structure and function is well understood.

The amount of oxygen that can be directly dissolved in blood is very small. Only 3 milliliters (mL) of oxygen can be dissolved in 1000 mL (1 L) of blood. The amount of dissolved oxygen is limited both by the fact that oxygen is not very soluble in water or blood and by the amount of oxygen available in the atmosphere. More than 98% of the oxygen in the blood is bound to hemoglobin molecules.

THE STRUCTURE OF HEMOGLOBIN
Each red blood cell is estimated to hold about 280 million hemoglobin molecules. Hemoglobin is composed of a protein component called **globin** and a red pigment component called **heme**. The heme gives blood its red color. At the center of each

heme group is an iron (Fe^{2+}) atom to which a single oxygen molecule can bind. Each hemoglobin molecule contains four heme groups, so one hemoglobin molecule can bind a total of four oxygen molecules.

Each globin molecule consists of four separate polypeptide chains bound together. Each chain has a heme group attached to it (Figure 4.1). Two of the polypeptide chains consist of identical alpha chains, and two chains are identical beta chains. The chains are held together by chemical bonds that stabilize the hemoglobin structure.

Two different genes code for these globin proteins, one for the alpha chain and one for the beta chain. The hemoglobin of human fetuses contains an alternate globin protein. Instead of two alpha and two beta chains, fetal hemoglobin contains two alpha and two gamma chains. As a result, fetal hemoglobin binds oxygen more tightly than adult hemoglobin does. This important property of fetal blood allows for the transfer of oxygen from maternal to fetal hemoglobin within the placenta.

Another variation in human globin genes occurs with sickle-cell disease, also known as sickle-cell anemia. In this hereditary disorder, the substitution of one amino acid for another in the beta chains changes the structure of the chains and leads to a variety of symptoms, some of which can be very debilitating (see box on page 42).

HEMOGLOBIN AND THE COOPERATIVE BINDING OF OXYGEN

The ability of a protein to bind a substance is described as its **affinity** for the substance. Where the affinity is higher, the substance will be more strongly bound to the protein. For example, fetal hemoglobin has a higher affinity for oxygen than adult hemoglobin due to the presence of the gamma chains. Therefore, fetal hemoglobin binds oxygen more tightly than adult hemoglobin, all other factors being equal.

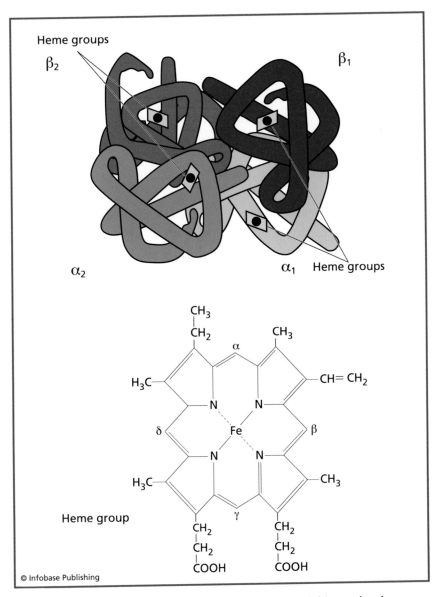

Figure 4.1 Structure of hemoglobin. Hemoglobin molecules consist of four polypeptide chains, two alpha (α) and two beta (ß) chains, with one heme group bound at the center of each chain. The heme groups each have an iron atom, Fe^{2+}, to which a molecule of oxygen can bind. Hence, each hemoglobin molecule can bind four oxygen molecules.

The binding of one oxygen molecule to one of the heme groups results in a slight shape, or *conformational*, change in the globin of hemoglobin. This slight change in the structure of the globin chain is transmitted to the remaining three chains, increasing their affinity for oxygen. In other words, the binding of one oxygen molecule makes it easier to bind the next three oxygen molecules, a characteristic known as **cooperative binding**.

The relationship of cooperative binding to oxygen binding can best be described by examining a **saturation curve** for hemoglobin. A saturation curve compares the availability of oxygen in the surrounding environment with the degree, in percent, that the hemoglobin molecules are saturated with oxygen (Figure 4.2). For example, a saturation of 100% would indicate that the hemoglobin molecules are fully saturated with oxygen—that is, all four heme groups have oxygen molecules bound to them and there are no unoccupied binding sites. Hemoglobin with no bound oxygen, also known as **deoxyhemoglobin**, is 0% saturated. If, on average, one of four sites on the hemoglobin molecules is occupied with oxygen, the hemoglobin solution is 25% saturated.

Oxygen availability is measured by physiologists using units of pressure. In Figure 4.2 and throughout this book, pressure is stated in millimeters of mercury (mm Hg). The pressure of oxygen in the atmosphere or in a solution is expressed as a partial pressure (since it is not the only gas present). For this reason, the symbol for the partial pressure of oxygen is PO_2. At sea level, the PO_2 of the atmosphere is about 160 mm Hg. The PO_2 of the air within the human lung is about 100 mm Hg.

If there were no cooperative binding effect, the relationship between the amount of oxygen in the environment (the PO_2) and the amount of O_2 bound to hemoglobin (the percent saturation) would be linear. Instead, once the degree of saturation reaches 25%, small increases in oxygen availability result in greater amounts of oxygen bound to hemoglobin. For

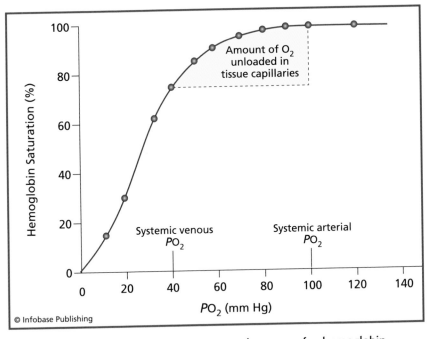

Figure 4.2 A typical oxygen saturation curve for hemoglobin. Note the sigmoidal, or S, shape of the curve, which is due to the cooperative binding of oxygen. Resting partial pressure (*P*) values for the lungs and systemic tissues are indicated on the graph. Typically, at rest, only 25% of the oxygen bound to hemoglobin is released to the tissues. The remaining 75% represents a circulating oxygen reserve.

example, if the starting PO_2 level is 10 mm Hg, an increase in PO_2 of 10 mm Hg results in an increase of about 15% saturation (from 15 to 30%). If, however, the starting PO_2 is 20 mm Hg, an increase of 10 mm Hg results in an increase of about 30% saturation (from 30 to 60%). Since hemoglobin also unloads, or releases, oxygen to tissues that need it, we can also look at this same relationship a different way. A small drop in PO_2 results in more oxygen being unloaded to the tissues.

Within a certain range, small changes in oxygen availability result in relatively large changes in the oxygen saturation of hemoglobin. Why is this important? Those tissues that are more metabolically active at any given time will have consumed more oxygen using the process of **cellular respiration** to make **ATP**. These tissues will have lower PO_2 levels than other, less active, tissues and will, therefore, receive more oxygen because more will be released.

To summarize, the ability of hemoglobin to bind oxygen, or its affinity for oxygen, increases when one oxygen molecule binds to one of the heme groups. This enhanced ability to bind oxygen is caused by a conformational change in the globin, or protein, component of hemoglobin. This property of hemoglobin, called cooperative binding, is responsible for the S-shaped saturation curve. Within a certain range, small changes in PO_2 levels result in larger changes in the O_2 affinity, a property of hemoglobin that is very physiologically important and is discussed later in this chapter.

The Transport of Oxygen by Hemoglobin

In a healthy human at rest, the typical PO_2 levels, or oxygen concentrations, encountered by hemoglobin as it travels through the bloodstream are highest in the lungs, where oxygen is taken up from the atmosphere. The PO_2 of the blood leaving the lungs is typically 100 mm Hg at sea level. The lowest PO_2 levels encountered by hemoglobin are in the tissues, where oxygen is consumed by cellular respiration. The most metabolically active tissues, such as the kidneys and heart, consume the most oxygen, and, as a consequence, they will have the lowest PO_2 levels. On average, however, tissue PO_2 levels are about 40 mm Hg.

Therefore, in a resting healthy human at sea level, hemoglobin that is circulating travels through PO_2 environments that vary from 40 to 100 mm Hg. To determine the degree to which hemoglobin is saturated with oxygen at both of these pressures, it is necessary to examine the oxygen saturation curve (Figure 4.3a). Hemoglobin entering the lungs from the tissues, where PO_2 levels are 40 mm Hg, will be 75%

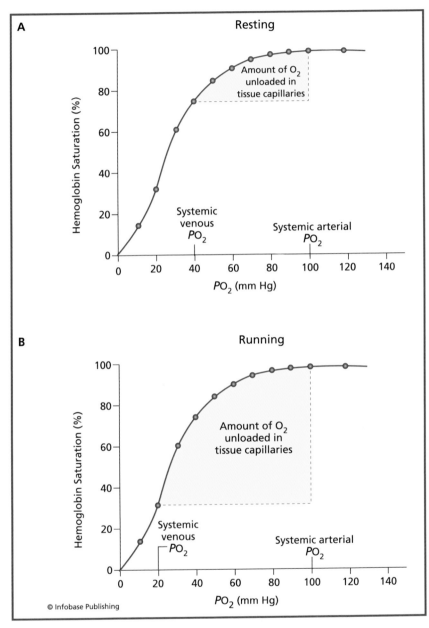

Figure 4.3 A comparison of the degree of oxygen saturation of hemoglobin in a person at rest (a) and while running (b). As shown in (b), when the partial pressure of oxygen in body tissues drops, significantly more oxygen is released by hemoglobin, illustrating the use of the oxygen reserve.

saturated with oxygen; thus, on average, three out of the four binding sites will be bonded to oxygen. Upon reaching the lungs where the PO_2 levels are 100 mm Hg, the hemoglobin molecules become 100% saturated with oxygen.

As these saturated hemoglobin molecules travel to the respiring tissues, where the PO_2 levels are 40 mm Hg, some of the oxygen is unloaded (about 25%) and the remaining 75% stays bound to hemoglobin. This remaining oxygen serves as an oxygen reserve in the blood, which is available when activity increases and the rate of cellular respiration increases.

For example, when a person begins to run, the leg muscles, heart, and respiratory muscles go from a resting state to a more active state. Because the rate of muscular contraction in these organs increases with running, the rates of cellular respiration must increase to provide adequate amounts of ATP to fuel this activity. More oxygen will be needed for cellular respiration. As more oxygen is consumed in these active tissues, their PO_2 levels begin to drop below 40 mm Hg. Observe what happens to the oxygen reserve in hemoglobin when it encounters these lower PO_2 environments (Figure 4.3).

If, for example, the PO_2 levels in certain leg muscles drop from the resting level of 40 mm Hg to 20 mm Hg with activity, hemoglobin encountering a PO_2 of 20 mm Hg will unload 70% of its oxygen, in contrast to the 25% seen in the previous example. If we compare the two conditions with respect to the degree of saturation of hemoglobin, we can begin to appreciate the physiological importance of the S-shaped saturation curve. When hemoglobin that is fully saturated encounters a tissue PO_2 of 40 mm Hg—a difference of 100–40, or 60 mm Hg—it unloads only 25% of its oxygen. However, when hemoglobin encounters a tissue PO_2 level of 20 mm Hg—a difference of 100–20, or 80 mm Hg—it unloads fully 70% of the oxygen that it carries.

Below 40 mm Hg (the PO_2 of tissues at rest), small changes in tissue PO_2 levels cause greater amounts of oxygen to be released by hemoglobin. Hemoglobin is most responsive to the needs of active tissues. The circulating oxygen reserve can be readily tapped when needed. It should also be understood how hemoglobin traveling to a metabolically active tissue, like a contracting muscle, will lose more oxygen to that tissue. If, however, that same molecule had happened to circulate to a less active tissue (for example, in part of the digestive system of someone who is running), less oxygen would have been released and the hemoglobin molecule would return to the lungs at a higher degree of saturation.

HEMOGLOBIN AND THE BOHR EFFECT

The unique S-shaped saturation curve is not the only characteristic of hemoglobin that contributes to its ability to release more oxygen to metabolically active tissues. In addition to responding to changing PO_2 levels, hemoglobin responds to the presence of other tissue factors that reflect the level of metabolic activity. One such factor is the carbon dioxide level. Remember that as the rate of cellular respiration increases, the production of CO_2, a waste product of cellular respiration, also increases. Thus, increased cellular activity results in both increased O_2 consumption and decreased PO_2 levels as well as increased PCO_2 levels due to increased production of carbon dioxide.

The structure of hemoglobin is sensitive to PCO_2 levels. When circulating hemoglobin encounters an environment with elevated PCO_2 levels, the CO_2 decreases hemoglobin's affinity for oxygen, and oxygen is released to the tissue. CO_2 reduces hemoglobin's ability to bind O_2 both directly and indirectly. CO_2 can bind directly to the amino-terminal ends of the alpha and beta chains of the globin molecules. The binding of CO_2 to hemoglobin causes a conformational change, reducing hemoglobin's hold on oxygen and, as a consequence, oxygen is released. The sensitivity of hemoglobin to PCO_2 levels can be illustrated on a saturation curve (Figure 4.5). The curve on the left, with a PCO_2 level of 45 mm Hg, represents the carbon dioxide concentrations that hemoglobin might encounter in the lungs. The curve on

(continues on page 44)

SICKLE-CELL DISEASE

Sickle-cell disease, or sickle-cell anemia, was the first genetic disorder to be understood at the molecular level. As early as 1949, scientists observed that the hemoglobin molecules of healthy individuals differed from those of sickle-cell patients. Later, it was determined that the mutation that causes this disease resides in the gene (called the mutated sickling gene) that determines the structure of the beta chain of the globin component of hemoglobin. A difference in a single DNA nucleotide results in the substitution of the amino acid glutamic acid for valine, altering just one of the 146 amino acids that compose the beta chain.

The sickling gene results in hemoglobin that crystallizes at low oxygen concentrations, deforming the typical biconcave shape of the red blood cell into a sickle shape (Figure 4.4). The deformed red blood cells become lodged in the tiny capillaries, obstructing blood flow and oxygen delivery to tissues and causing pain and organ damage. A sickling crisis can be triggered in individuals with sickle-cell disease when the oxygen level of their blood is low—for example, at high altitude or with increased physical activity. Deformed red blood cells are removed from circulation and destroyed by the liver, resulting in a decreased number of circulating red blood cells, otherwise known as anemia.

Sickle-cell disease is an example of incomplete dominance, a form of inheritance in which an intermediate form of the trait is observed. In the case of incomplete dominance, a person who is heterozygous (that is, has one normal version of the gene and one sickling version) is usually healthy, but may have some symptoms of the disease when experiencing reduced blood oxygen levels.

Sickle-cell disease is also of interest to evolutionary biologists. Malaria is a devastating disease that ravages many tropical regions of the world. It is caused by the parasite *Plasmodium falciparum*, which is carried by the *Anopheles gambiae* mosquito. The mosquito transmits the parasite to the humans it bites. Once in the bloodstream, the malarial parasite enters the red blood cells and is transported throughout the body.

The British geneticist Anthony Allison observed that the regions of Africa where the malarial parasite was most prevalent

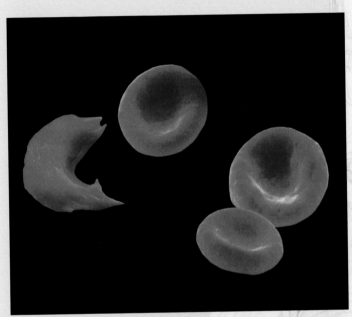

Figure 4.4 A mutation in the gene that determines the structure of the beta chain of the globin component of hemoglobin results in the deformation of the red blood cell. A typical biconcave red blood cell is shown on the right, while the cell on the left shows the sickle shape of a red blood cell found in people who have sickle-cell disease.

coincided with the regions where a large percentage of the human population was heterozygous for the sickling gene. It appears that possessing one copy of the sickling gene protects against malarial infection. Those populations with a higher frequency of the trait tend to have milder, less devastating cases of malaria. The sickling gene and its effect on red blood cells render these cells uninhabitable by the malarial parasite, significantly reducing the degree of infection.

With information on the human genome and the genomes of *Plasmodium falciparum* and *Anopheles gambiae*, scientists hope to identify an effective means of reducing malaria's debilitating effect on human populations.

(continued from page 41)

the right represents a PCO_2 level of about 50 mm Hg, levels of carbon dioxide that a hemoglobin molecule might encounter in a typical body tissue. You can see that the saturation curve for hemoglobin shifts to the right with higher and higher PCO_2 levels, a phenomenon called the **Bohr effect**.

This shift of the oxygen saturation curve to the right in the Bohr effect represents a decrease in the affinity of hemoglobin for oxygen with increasing PCO_2. What is the physiological significance of this shift? Whenever you are trying to assess the consequences of any shift in the saturation curve for hemoglobin, it is best to start by choosing one PO_2 level for

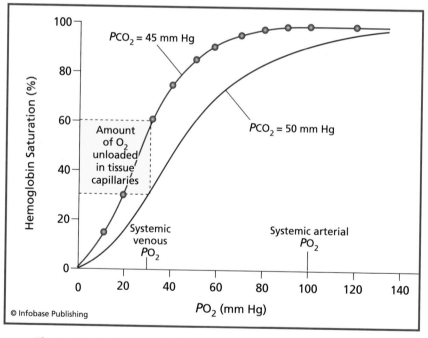

Figure 4.5 An increase in the partial pressure of carbon dioxide in the surrounding tissues results in a shift to the right of the oxygen saturation curve, indicating a decrease in hemoglobin's affinity for oxygen.

comparison. For this example, compare two saturation curves at a PO_2 of 30 mm Hg. Using the saturation curve at a PCO_2 of 50 mm Hg, a typical value for a body tissue, we can determine that in the presence of a PO_2 of 30 mm Hg, hemoglobin will unload 40% of the oxygen it carries; that is, it will remain 60% saturated with oxygen. However, in the presence of a PCO_2 of 50 mm Hg, it unloads even more oxygen, 70%, such that only 30% remains. More oxygen is released to environments with higher PCO_2 levels. In this way, hemoglobin is responsive to the PCO_2 levels as well as the PO_2 levels of the tissues.

Other factors associated with exercise promote the unloading of oxygen from hemoglobin to those tissues that are most in need of it. Muscle that is being exercised experiences increased temperatures due to the increased metabolic activity and a decrease in pH due to the enhanced production of carbon dioxide and lactic acid. Both increased temperature and decreased pH promote the unloading of oxygen from hemoglobin to the exercising muscle cells.

To summarize, increased CO_2 levels, decreased pH (or increased acidity), and increased temperature are all factors that result in a decrease in hemoglobin's affinity for oxygen, thereby promoting oxygen release to the tissues. This is advantageous, since an increase in the rate of cellular respiration produces more CO_2, hence more H^+ and more heat.

CONNECTIONS

Hemoglobin, found in red blood cells, is the respiratory pigment that binds and transports oxygen in the blood. Its protein component consists of four polypeptide chains, two alpha and two beta chains, held together by chemical bonds. Each polypeptide chain has a heme molecule with a binding site for

(continues on page 46)

(continued from page 45)

oxygen at its Fe^{2+} (iron) center. Therefore, each hemoglobin molecule can bind four oxygen molecules.

The binding of one oxygen molecule increases the affinity of hemoglobin for oxygen, making it easier to bind the next three oxygen molecules, a phenomenon known as cooperative binding. As a result, hemoglobin's saturation curve, which describes how its affinity for oxygen changes with the PO_2 of the surrounding environment, is S-shaped rather than linear.

Increased metabolic activity (that is, an increased rate of cellular respiration) results in an increase in carbon dioxide production, increased acidity (a decrease in pH), and increased temperature. Such changes reduce the affinity of hemoglobin for oxygen, causing a shift to the right of the oxygen-saturation curve, thereby increasing the amount of oxygen released to the tissues.

5

Anatomy of the Circulatory System

As described in Chapter 2, the human circulatory system is divided into two separate circuits: the systemic circuit and the pulmonary circuit (Figure 5.1). Blood travels through a similar sequence of blood vessels in the two circuits. In both circuits, blood is pumped out of the heart into large arteries, which divide and subdivide to form smaller and smaller vessels until the blood enters the smallest arteries, which are called the **arterioles**. From the arterioles, blood passes into the smallest vessels, the capillaries, which are the sites of exchange of material with the body's cells. From the capillaries, the vessels merge into larger and larger vessels, forming **venules** and then veins. The veins carry the blood back to the heart. The left side of the heart propels blood throughout the systemic circuit, which supplies the entire body. The right side of the heart propels blood through the pulmonary circuit to the lungs for the exchange of gas with the atmosphere, before returning it to the heart.

In this chapter, you will examine the anatomy of the heart and blood vessels. You will also learn about two common circulatory diseases afflicting millions of Americans: atherosclerosis and **myocardial infarction,** or **heart attack**.

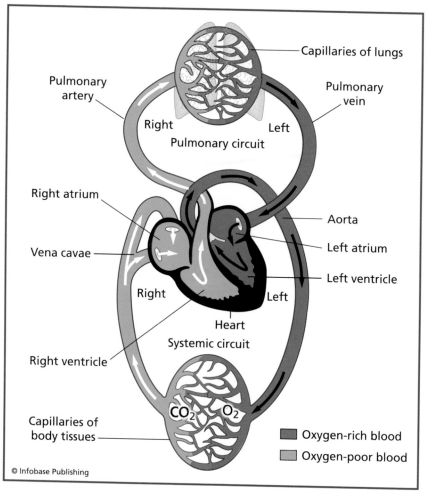

Figure 5.1   An overview of the pulmonary and systemic circuits of the human circulatory system. The chambers of the right side of the heart pump blood into the pulmonary circuit, while the left chambers move blood into the systemic circuit. For both circuits, blood leaving the heart travels through arteries, then arterioles and capillaries. Blood leaving the capillaries passes into venules and then veins before returning to the heart. In the pulmonary circuit, gas exchange occurs in the capillaries in the lungs. In the systemic circuit, gas exchange occurs in the capillaries of the body tissues. In this diagram, blue represents deoxygenated blood, and red represents oxygenated blood. Capillary blood is shown in purple.

ANATOMY OF THE HEART

The heart beats steadily from early in embryonic development until death. The heart of someone who lives for 75 years will beat an average of 75 times per minute, and, by the time its owner dies, it will have beat a total of 3 billion times and pumped more than 53 million gallons (200 million L) of blood.

The heart is located in the chest, or thoracic cavity, with the lungs. It lies slightly left of the midline of the body. Because the heart takes up more space on the left side of the chest cavity, the left lung has two lobes, compared to the three lobes of the right lung. The heart is surrounded by

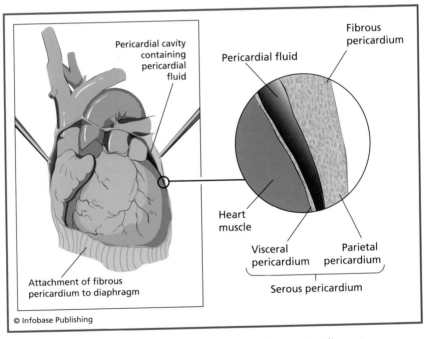

Pericardial cavity containing pericardial fluid

Pericardial fluid

Fibrous pericardium

Heart muscle

Visceral pericardium

Parietal pericardium

Serous pericardium

Attachment of fibrous pericardium to diaphragm

© Infobase Publishing

Figure 5.2 The heart is surrounded by the pericardium, two layers of membrane separated by pericardial fluid. The fluid helps lubricate the heart and reduce friction. The tough outer membrane of the pericardium (fibrous pericardium) helps keep the heart in place during its vigorous beating actions.

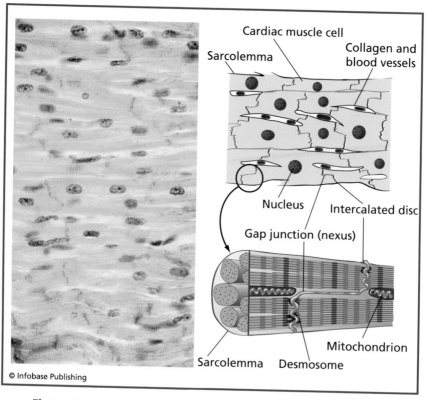

Cardiac muscle cell
Sarcolemma
Collagen and blood vessels
Nucleus
Intercalated disc
Gap junction (nexus)
Mitochondrion
Sarcolemma   Desmosome

© Infobase Publishing

Figure 5.3 Cardiac muscle cells are smaller than skeletal muscle cells and are connected through structures known as intercalated discs. Desmosomes, or adhesion molecules, help to hold the cardiac cells together during contractions. Gap junctions allow for synchronization of heart contractions. A photograph of actual cardiac muscle is shown on the left. The illustrations on the right depict the components of cardiac muscle.

the **pericardium**, a protective covering that anchors the heart to the diaphragm and large blood vessels (Figure 5.2). The pericardium consists of two membranes with fluid between. The pericardial fluid lubricates the heart and reduces friction during beating. The tough outer pericardial membrane protects the outer surface of the heart and helps keep the heart in position while it beats.

The walls of the heart are made up of **cardiac muscle**. Although all muscle tissue is specialized for contraction, cardiac muscle has some characteristics that differ from the skeletal muscle that moves the joints and that reflect its unique function as a pump. For example, individual cardiac muscle cells are smaller than skeletal muscle cells and they contain a single nucleus (Figure 5.3). Cardiac muscle cells also differ from skeletal muscle in that they are connected to each other through regions known as **intercalated discs**. A high density of adhesion molecules known as **desmosomes** keep the cells tightly attached to each other in these regions, ensuring that the forces generated during the beating actions of the heart do not rip apart the heart muscle. **Gap junctions** allow ions to move from one cardiac cell to another, and, as you will learn in Chapter 6, these junctions help the heart muscle to synchronize its actions.

The human heart possesses four chambers that fill with blood: two upper **atria** (plural for **atrium**) and two lower **ventricles** (Figure 5.4). The right side of the heart, consisting of the right atrium and right ventricle, is separated from the left side of the heart by a wall, or *septum*. The right and left side of the heart may beat as one unit, but they are completely separate from each other with respect to the blood that they contain. Both the right and left atria are separated from their respective ventricles by **atrioventricular (AV) valves**, folds of tough tissue that open in one direction only.

The atria receive blood returning to the heart from the lungs and from the body tissues and then pump that blood into the ventricles. The ventricles are the more muscular pumps of the heart, because they must generate enough force to propel the blood out into circulation against the pressures existing in the two circuits. The muscular walls of the atria are thinner than those of the ventricles, reflecting the fact that they do not have to generate the high forces required of the ventricles. Similarly, because the left ventricle must generate enough force

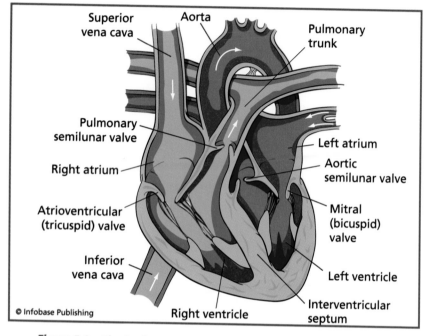

Figure 5.4 The basic anatomy of the human heart includes the atria and ventricles, the attached major blood vessels, and the semilunar and atrioventricular valves. Recall that the right side of the heart sends blood to the lungs, and the left side supplies the entire body. Note the thickness of the left ventricular wall.

to overcome the higher pressure existing in the systemic circuit and propel blood for longer distances, its muscular walls are thicker than those of the right ventricle. The right ventricle supplies the pulmonary circuit, where the distance traveled by the blood is short and blood pressure is lower.

The muscular walls of the atria are easily stretched and can accommodate large volumes of blood returning to the heart. The right atrium receives blood returning from the systemic circuit via two large veins: the **superior vena cava**, which drains all regions above the heart, and the **inferior vena cava**, which collects blood returning from the lower body regions. The **AV**

valve separating the right atrium and ventricle is sometimes called the **tricuspid valve** because it is composed of three flaps of tissue. This valve opens only when blood pressure in the atria exceeds ventricular pressure, thus preventing any backflow into the atria when the pressure gradient is reversed. The left AV valve, or **bicuspid valve**, serves a similar function between the left atrium and ventricle, but consists of two flaps instead of three.

The cone-shaped left and right ventricles are similar in design. The right ventricle pushes blood out into the pulmonary circuit through a **pulmonary semilunar valve**, which separates the ventricular chamber from the pulmonary trunk. This valve opens when ventricular pressure exceeds pressure in the pulmonary artery; otherwise it remains closed. In a similar fashion, the **aortic semilunar valve** separates the left ventricle from the **ascending aorta**. This valve only opens when left ventricular pressure is greater than pressure in the aorta. Both semilunar valves prevent blood from flowing back into the heart once it has had been forced out into circulation.

The importance of the AV and semilunar valves is underscored by conditions that lead to their malfunction. Rheumatic fever, a condition that may develop after an infection with *Streptococcus*, can lead to valve dysfunction even decades after the infection occurred. Some individuals are born with malformations of their heart valves. Regardless of the cause, malfunctioning valves can cause debilitating reductions in cardiac function.

Every year, nearly 300,000 patients require valve replacement surgery. Valve replacement involves open-heart surgery and the installation of either a mechanical valve, made of metal or plastic, or a biological valve obtained from a human or other animal, most often a cow or pig. The mechanical valves do not wear out, but do cause clotting so that patients must take blood thinners for life. The biological valves may wear out over time, especially if the patient is young. Recently, stem cells were used to create a heart valve substitute. These cells were harvested from bone marrow, treated so that they developed into heart valve cells, and placed on a collagen scaffold to form a valve. While it will likely be years before these stem cell-generated heart valves will be implanted into humans, scientists are very

CORONARY-ARTERY DISEASE AND HEART ATTACK

Coronary arteries bring oxygen-rich blood to the hard-working heart muscle. The blockage of these arteries, as well as others in the body, most often arises from a condition known as atherosclerosis, sometimes called "hardening of the arteries." With this disease, calcified fatty deposits, or plaques, build up in the inner lining of these arteries. If the plaques grow large enough to reduce blood flow, the heart's access to oxygen and nutrients may be affected and its ability to function impaired. If a plaque ruptures, the consequences can be even more severe because the blood clot that forms as a result of the rupture may block the artery completely or break free and lodge in a smaller artery and block the blood flow there.

The sequence of events that leads to atherosclerosis is very complex and not completely understood by scientists. It appears to start with some kind of injury to the innermost layer of the artery, often due to high blood pressure, smoking, or diabetes. Once the damage has occurred, platelets, fats (in the form of triglycerides), cholesterol, calcium, and other substances all get incorporated into the injury site, shrinking the diameter of the artery and blocking the blood flow.

While atherosclerosis can affect any of the blood vessels, the coronary arteries, the aorta, and the leg arteries are the most common vessels to be affected. If the flow of blood to a region of the heart is interrupted for more than a few minutes, there may be permanent damage to the portion of the heart muscle supplied by that vessel. Such an event is known as a myocardial infarction, or heart attack. The extent and severity of the damage determines encouraged by this result and even expect that soon they will be able to grow a complete heart by using stem cells.

THE CORONARY ARTERIES

One might think that since the heart is always filled with blood that it would not need its own blood supply, but this

whether the individual who suffered the attack will live or die. Warning signs of an impending heart attack may include **angina**, or chest pain. People suffering from angina often experience the pain when they exert themselves. As their level of activity increases, the heart works harder to compensate and is more likely to become oxygen-deprived.

The risk factors associated with atherosclerosis include high levels of "bad" cholesterol, or LDL (low-density lipoprotein), and low levels of HDL (high-density lipoprotein), or "good" cholesterol. Cholesterol-lowering drugs, like statins, are often used to help prevent and reverse plaque formation. There is increased incidence of atherosclerosis for older individuals, for people with high blood pressure or diabetes, and for those who smoke, drink excessively, are obese, or are inactive. Genetics and stress also appear to play a role. Medical practitioners use blood tests, **electrocardiograms** (also known as **ECGs** or **EKGs**), stress tests, and techniques that visualize the blood flow through the coronary or other arteries to diagnose the presence of atherosclerosis.

Clogged coronary arteries can be opened by using **angioplasty**. Plaques can be removed or pressed into the arterial wall by using an inflated balloon. If these procedures fail to increase blood flow to the heart muscle adequately, then coronary bypass surgery may be needed. In this treatment, small vessels, like the great saphenous vein of the leg, are removed to replace a diseased section of a coronary artery. A quadruple bypass surgery means that four separate coronary arteries are bypassed using this technique during a single operation. Bypass surgery has become safer and fairly routine and is successful at improving heart function and reducing angina in most individuals with coronary artery disease.

is not so. The heart is a hardworking muscle and therefore needs a constant and ample supply of oxygen and fuel, a task accomplished by the coronary arteries. Recall that the left ventricle pumps blood out into the systemic circuit through the aortic semilunar valve and into the ascending aorta. The right and left coronary arteries branch off from the base of the ascending aorta to bring oxygen-rich blood to their respective sides of the heart. Blood flow through these arteries can increase up to nine times above the resting rate during intensive exercise when the heart is pumping maximally. The coronary arteries of a large number of Americans are diseased, reducing the ability of their hearts to function properly.

THE BLOOD VESSELS

The circulatory system consists of the heart, blood, and blood vessels. We have just examined the structure and function of the heart, the muscular pump that provides the force to circulate blood throughout the body. Previously, we discussed the composition of blood, the fluid medium that transports oxygen, nutrients, and water to our cells and removes wastes. Now, we will examine the types of blood vessels found in the human circulatory system.

Within each of the two circuits, there are five basic types of blood vessels: arteries, arterioles, capillaries, venules, and veins. The various types of vessels differ in their structures and functions (Figure 5.5).

When blood is first ejected from the heart, it enters large **arteries** that immediately begin to branch into medium-sized and then into small arteries. The arteries receive the pressurized blood from the heart and distribute it to all of the body's tissues, including the heart itself. Arterial walls are thick because they are very muscular (Figure 5.5a). The larger arteries have elastic walls that can withstand the large changes in blood pressure that accompany the actions of the heart.

These vessels are designed for the efficient transport of blood away from the heart.

The medium-sized arteries distribute blood to the skeletal muscles and major organs. These arteries, in general, have a thinner layer of muscle, although the difference in structure from the larger arteries is subtle. Overall, with increasing distance from the heart, the diameters of the arteries decrease; also, the amount of muscle in the arterial wall decreases as the arteries become smaller.

Arterioles are small arteries that have an inner layer of smooth muscle cells. These vessels play the more critical role in determining blood pressure. When arterioles receive a signal to relax, or dilate—a process known as **vasodilation**—there is an increase in their diameter with a corresponding decrease in blood pressure. Conversely, when stimulated to decrease their diameter, or **vasoconstrict**, they can initiate a profound increase in blood pressure. For this reason, the arterioles are called the **resistance vessels**. When they are constricted, they resist blood flow and increase blood pressure.

Arterioles subdivide to form capillaries, the smallest vessels and the sites for the exchange of materials between the blood and the body tissues, in the case of the systemic circuit, and the blood and lung tissue, in the case of the pulmonary circuit. Capillary walls must be very thin to minimize the diffusion distance for substances like oxygen, carbon dioxide, and glucose. The typical capillary wall consists only of a single layer of endothelium surrounded by a thin basement membrane (Figure 5.5b). The diameter of these vessels is so small that red blood cells can barely squeeze through in single file. The rate of blood flow through the capillaries is quite slow, which permits ample time for the exchange of materials with the tissues.

Capillaries are organized into networks called **capillary beds**. Blood may be restricted from entering a capillary bed if rings of smooth muscle, called **precapillary sphincters,**

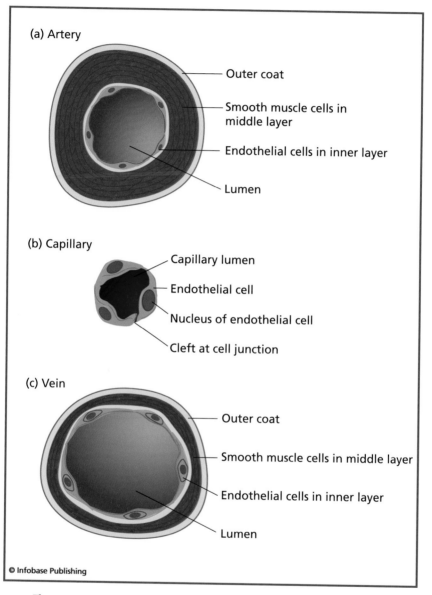

(a) Artery

Outer coat

Smooth muscle cells in middle layer

Endothelial cells in inner layer

Lumen

(b) Capillary

Capillary lumen

Endothelial cell

Nucleus of endothelial cell

Cleft at cell junction

(c) Vein

Outer coat

Smooth muscle cells in middle layer

Endothelial cells in inner layer

Lumen

© Infobase Publishing

Figure 5.5 Structure of blood vessels. (a) Cross section of an artery. (b) Cross section of a capillary. (c) Cross section of a vein.

are constricted. When the sphincters are relaxed, blood flows into the bed. In this way, blood flow to specific body regions can be adjusted based on the need for oxygen. The regulation of this change in flow to a region is discussed in Chapter 7.

Capillaries empty into venules, which are small-diameter veins. The venules merge into medium-sized veins, which then merge into large-diameter veins. Veins return blood to the heart. They differ in a number of ways from arteries; for example, the walls of veins are thinner and the lumens are larger, characteristics that render veins collapsible (Figure 5.5c). Veins serve as **capacitance vessels** for the circulatory system, holding up to 65% of the body's entire blood volume at any one time.

In addition, large veins have valves that keep blood flowing toward the heart (Figure 5.6). These valves work in a fashion similar to the heart valves; that is, they only allow blood to flow in one direction. When the blood pressure is greater below the valve, the valve is forced open and the blood moves closer to the heart. This change in pressure could happen, for example, when a leg muscle contracts and squeezes the vein. When blood pressure on both sides of the valve is equal, or when it is greater above the valve, the valve remains closed, so there is no backflow of blood, despite the forces of gravity or a pressure gradient that might favor such backflow.

The presence of these valves is especially important in the large leg veins when someone is standing up. The blood returning to the heart is under very low pressure and is moving against the force of gravity. The valves help prevent blood from pooling in the lower extremities under such circumstances, although periodic contractions of the skeletal muscles are required to squeeze the veins to push the blood past the valves.

THE PATH OF THE BLOOD THROUGH THE CIRCULATORY SYSTEM

We have now completed separate discussions of the structures of the heart and blood vessels. One of the best ways to understand the overall design of the human circulatory system is to take a ride with a red blood cell through the entire circuit. The journey will start in the left ventricle, the larger muscular chamber of the left side of the heart, and follow a red blood cell as it circulates and returns to this starting point.

When the heart beats, the red blood cell is forcibly ejected from the left ventricle into the aorta, the largest artery in the body. From there, the blood cell travels into one of many large arteries, which then branch into progressively smaller arteries. Hence, each vessel the red blood cell enters will eventually lead to multiple exit points as it branches. Soon, the red blood cell moves from a small systemic artery into a systemic arteriole with a smaller diameter. The arteriole leads to a systemic capillary bed in some tissue in the body where the vessels are so small that the red blood cell can barely squeeze through.

In this systemic capillary, the red blood cell gives up some of its load of oxygen (O_2) molecules to nearby cells for use in the process of cellular respiration. Carbon dioxide (CO_2), a waste product of cellular respiration, diffuses from these cells into the blood cell. After this exchange of gases, the blood cell enters a venule, then a small vein, and then a larger vein. Eventually, the blood cell reaches one of the large veins that return the oxygen-poor blood into the right atrium. This is the end of the systemic circuit.

The pulmonary circuit, where the red blood cell once again becomes oxygenated, begins when the blood enters the right atrium of the heart. From the right atrium, it is pumped into the right ventricle and then into the pulmonary arteries, which carry it to the lungs. Again, there is a significant degree of branching of first the larger and then the smaller pulmonary arteries. The red blood cell progresses from a small pulmonary arteriole into a pulmonary capillary, which is wrapped around a small portion of the lung surface. The carbon dioxide diffuses out of the capillary and into the air within the lung, while oxygen is diffusing in the opposite

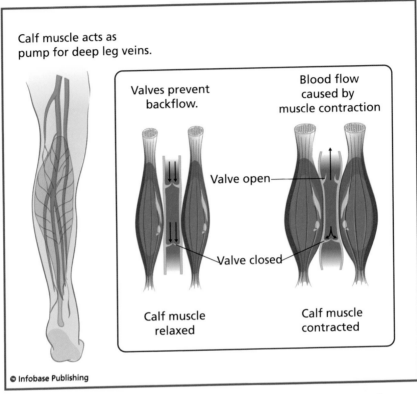

Calf muscle acts as pump for deep leg veins.

Valves prevent backflow.

Blood flow caused by muscle contraction

Valve open

Valve closed

Calf muscle relaxed

Calf muscle contracted

© Infobase Publishing

Figure 5.6 Blood pressures in the venous system are much lower than those in the arterial system. The larger veins have valves that prevent the backflow of blood and promote the return of blood to the heart. Contraction of the skeletal muscle surrounding a vein also helps to move the blood toward the heart.

direction and binding to the hemoglobin molecules packed within the red blood cell (recall that hemoglobin is a protein that helps red blood cells carry oxygen). Once again, pulmonary venules, followed by successively larger veins, collect the blood as it leaves its capillary bed. Soon after entering one of the large pulmonary veins, the blood cell is deposited into the left atrium and finally the left ventricle, where it first began its journey.

There is no rest for the red blood cell. For blood to accomplish its function, it must remain in motion. As soon as it becomes stationary, its store of oxygen and nutrients quickly becomes depleted and the cell becomes saturated with waste products. Other critical bodily functions can become disrupted. To keep the body's blood in motion, the heart pumps about 8,000 L (2,100 gallons) of blood per day. This is equivalent to 4,000 regular 2-liter soda bottles!

It is difficult to say how quickly an individual blood cell will travel through the circulatory system. It would depend on which specific body tissue the cell is circulating through. The flow through individual organs and tissues varies from minute to minute based on the changing oxygen demands of tissues and on the type and degree of activity taking place at that time. The total flow of blood through the system remains fairly constant and is typically about 5.25 L (1.39 gallons) per minute, close to the total volume of blood contained within the system.

CONNECTIONS

The heart is a powerful muscle that is divided into four blood-filled chambers: two atria and two ventricles. Valves separate the atria from the ventricles and the ventricles from the blood vessels they supply, ensuring that blood flows through the heart in only one direction. The right side of the heart pumps blood through the pulmonary circuit, where it becomes oxygenated in the capillaries of the lungs. The oxygenated blood is then returned to the left side of the heart and pumped out into the systemic circuit.

The heart beats constantly and requires an ample blood supply, which is provided by the coronary arteries. Coronary artery diseases, such as atherosclerosis, affect millions of Americans and put them at increased risk for myocardial infarctions, or heart attacks.

Blood leaving the heart passes through the arteries, arterioles, capillaries, venules, and, finally, the veins before returning to the heart. Each of these blood vessels possesses unique characteristics that support its function. Capillaries are organized into functional networks known as capillary beds and represent the site of gas exchange between the blood and the tissues.

6

Pumping Blood:
How the Heart Works

IN THE LAST CHAPTER, WE LEARNED ABOUT THE STRUCTURE of the the heart. It has four hollow chambers that fill with blood. Valves keep blood flowing in a single direction at all times through the heart and the remainder of the circulatory system. We also explored how the cardiac muscle cells are interconnected both physically, through the presence of strong adhesion molecules known as desmosomes, and functionally, through gap junctions.

This chapter discusses how the heart generates the pressures necessary to propel blood through the pulmonary and systemic circuits. The heart generates its own rhythm of beating, a rhythm that can be influenced by the nervous and endocrine systems. The heart pumps constantly and increases its efforts when necessary to accommodate changes in a person's activity level.

THE CONDUCTING SYSTEM OF THE HEART
Every time the heart beats, the atria and ventricles contract in sequence so that blood is forced out into circulation throughout the body. The cells responsible for initiating this coordinated contraction reside within the heart muscle itself (that is,

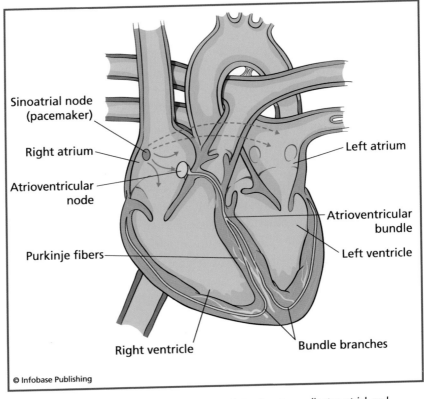

Sinoatrial node
(pacemaker)

Right atrium

Atrioventricular
node

Purkinje fibers

Left atrium

Atrioventricular
bundle

Left ventricle

Right ventricle

Bundle branches

© Infobase Publishing

Figure 6.1 The conducting system of the heart coordinates atrial and ventricular contractions. Pacemaker cells in the SA node of the right atrium generate a signal that is relayed to the AV node. From there, the signal is transmitted to the ventricles via the AV bundle, the bundle branches, and the Purkinje fibers.

the heart generates its own rhythm). A specialized system of cells then relays this stimulus quickly throughout the heart muscle. This conducting system of the heart consists of the following tissues: the sinoatrial node, the **atrioventricular node**, the atrioventricular bundle, and the Purkinje fibers. There also are a number of conducting cells involved in relaying this signal between each of these tissues.

The **sinoatrial (SA) node** is located in the wall of the right atrium (Figure 6.1). Within this structure are **pacemaker cells** that generate the heart rate. Pacemaker cells are **autorhythmic**; that is, they spontaneously initiate electrical impulses that appear as spikes in a recording of pacemaker activity (Figure 6.2). The rhythm of the impulses can be altered by input from the nervous system. The pacemaker cells do not maintain a stable resting state like most other cells do. These electrical impulses from the pacemaker rapidly spread to the other cells of the heart. After firing, the pacemaker cells rest for a brief period before generating a new wave of excitation.

This excitatory signal is rapidly relayed via conducting cells to the **atrioventricular (AV) node**, located at the base of the right atrium. At the same time, this signal is relayed throughout the right and left atrial muscle tissue and stimulates their contraction. The AV node slows the relay of the signal to the ventricles. This delay is critical to proper heart function. The atria need adequate time to contract down onto the volumes of blood within, force open the AV valves, and fill the ventricles before the ventricles begin to contract. Thus, the delay of the signal at the AV node ensures adequate filling of the ventricles. Because of this delay, the atria always contract before the ventricles, and while the ventricles are contracting, the atria are relaxing.

After the delay, the signal is then relayed from the AV node to the **AV bundle** located in the wall that separates the two ventricles. The AV bundle splits into two separate branches, one for each ventricle. As the branches reach the apex, or bottom tip, of the heart, they begin to branch into structures known as Purkinje fibers. The Purkinje fibers quickly spread the excitatory signal throughout the ventricular muscle tissue, stimulating contraction of the ventricles in a coordinated manner. Because the wave of contraction starts at the apex of the heart, blood is forced up and out of the semilunar valves and into the pulmonary and systemic circuits.

The coordination of atrial and ventricular contractions is necessary for efficient pumping of the blood. Any damage

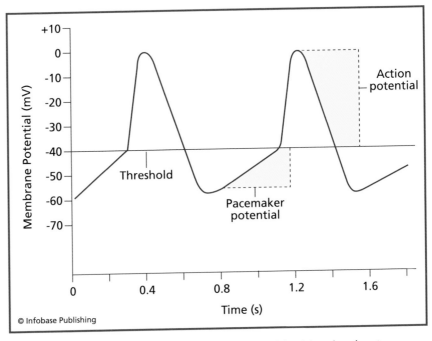

Figure 6.2 Pacemaker cells in the sinoatrial node of the right atrium do not remain in the resting state; instead, they spontaneously depolarize, moving the membrane potential toward threshold. Once the membrane potential reaches threshold, an excitatory signal is generated and then spread throughout the heart by the conducting system.

to the conducting system of heart leads to a loss of coordination and diminished heart function. Cardiac arrhythmias, or abnormalities in the conducting pathway of the heart, can be detected using an electrocardiogram, or ECG (sometimes abbreviated as EKG). With this procedure, electrodes are placed on key points of the body's surface to monitor the electrical activity of the heart.

Some of the more common features of an ECG recording are illustrated in Figure 6.3. The small **P wave** represents the spread of the excitatory signal throughout the atria. The **QRS complex** results from the ventricular depolarization, as the signal spreads via the AV bundle and the Purkinje fibers.

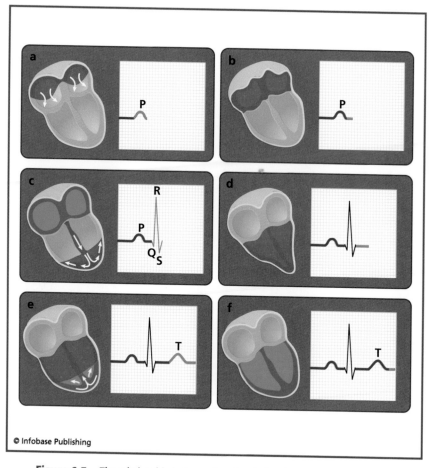

Figure 6.3   The relationship between the electrical activity of the heart and an electrocardiogram. The portions of the heart that are in depolarization and are therefore being stimulated to contract are shown in red. Green represents the initiation of repolarization (relaxation phase).

The **T wave** results from the repolarization, or return to the resting state, of the ventricles. The QRS complex masks the corresponding wave representing atrial repolarization. When these features are analyzed for any indication of arrhythmia, the size and shape of each curve is examined (see box, page 72). Any damage to the pacemaker cells of the SA node may require implantation of an electrical pacemaker to maintain the proper rhythm of heartbeats.

Because cardiac muscle cells are electrically coupled to each other via the gap junctions, areas of damaged heart muscle can also lead to a disruption of the conducting system of the heart. Myocardial infarctions, or heart attacks, due to the blockage or reduction of blood flow to an area of the heart can cause the muscle cells in that area to die and be replaced with scar tissue, which is nonconducting. Such a situation can be lethal because the entire heart rhythm may be disrupted, resulting in loss of blood pressure and blood flow. In the future, heart surgeons may be able to replace these patches of scar tissue by using stem cells to create new heart cells.

THE CARDIAC CYCLE

One complete cardiac cycle encompasses all of the events that occur in sequence from the start of one heartbeat until the start of the next. Examining this complete cycle will allow us to better understand how the electrical activity of the heart is coordinated with its contractile functions. Fluids, including blood, only move from one region to another if a pressure gradient exists. For blood to move from an atrium to a ventricle, for example, the pressure in the atrium must be higher than the pressure in the ventricle; otherwise, the valve between the two chambers remains closed. The flow of blood between these two chambers stops once the pressures are equal. Recall that the valves prevent blood from flowing from the ventricles back into atria once ventricular pressure exceeds atrial pressure.

The cardiac cycle is divided into two phases: the contraction phase, or **systole** (pronounced sis-toe-lee), and the relaxation phase, or **diastole** (pronounced die-as-toe-lee). Periods of systole are important for generating the pressures necessary for moving blood. Diastole is important to ensure that there is enough relaxation time for the chambers to refill with blood before the next contraction. The timing of atrial systole and ventricular systole is important. Atrial systole must precede ventricular systole to ensure adequate time to fill the ventricles fully before they begin contraction.

Figure 6.4 illustrates the events of the cardiac cycle. Using this diagram, the key features of an ECG can be correlated with the changes in pressure within the heart chambers and with changes in the blood volume within each of these chambers.

The P wave correlates with the start of atrial systole (contraction). The QRS complex is associated with the onset of ventricular systole and atrial diastole (relaxation). The T wave indicates the end of ventricular systole (and the start of ventricular diastole). There is a relatively long period when both the atria and ventricles are in diastole during which there is no wavelike electrical activity.

If the electrical events and phases are matched with pressure changes within the heart chambers, a picture of what occurs during atrial and ventricular systole begins to emerge. The left side of the heart must eject blood out of the heart against the high pressure that exists within the systemic circuit. This pressure, represented on the graph by the aortic pressure, varies between 90 and 120 mm Hg during the course of one cardiac cycle. After the QRS complex appears and ventricular systole starts, pressure begins to build within the ventricle as its muscular walls squeeze down on the volume of blood within. As soon as the pressure within the ventricle exceeds the pressure in the aorta, the aortic semilunar valve opens and blood is forcibly ejected into the aorta (causing aortic pressure to rise).

As the volume of blood decreases within the left ventricle, its pressure starts to decrease. Once ventricular pressure is below aortic pressure, the aortic semilunar valve closes, and no more blood is ejected. The ventricle then relaxes, allowing the relaxed heart to refill with blood.

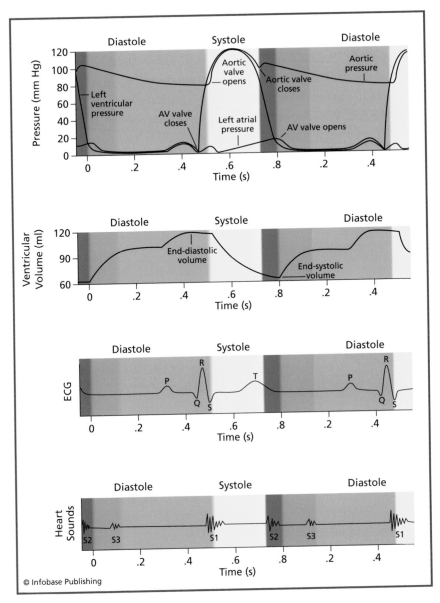

Figure 6.4   Changes in pressure and volume accompany the cardiac cycle. The events are shown in coordination with a typical electrocardiogram (ECG) recording and the major heart sounds as detected by a stethoscope. Two complete cardiac cycles are depicted.

The pressure changes in the right atrium and right ventricle are perfectly coordinated with the events in the left atrium and ventricle. The right and left sides of the heart contract and relax in concert. The difference between the right and left heart is the pressure against which they must eject their respective volumes of blood. While aortic pressure varies between 90 and 120 mm Hg, pulmonary arterial pressures are much lower, typically ranging from 10 to 25 mm Hg. When right ventricular pressure exceeds that of the pulmonary aorta, the pulmonary semilunar valve opens and blood is ejected into the pulmonary circuit.

IRREGULAR HEART RHYTHMS AND PACEMAKERS

Because an electrocardiogram (ECG) records the electrical activity of the heart, it can also be used to detect irregular heart rhythms. The ECG can determine, for example, whether the heart is beating too fast, a condition called **tachycardia**, or too slow, a condition called **bradycardia**, by measuring the amount of time elapsed from one QRS complex to the next.

A particularly dangerous form of tachycardia in the ventricles of the heart is known as *ventricular fibrillation*, or *ventricular flutter*. These forms of tachycardia typically occur when an area of the ventricle becomes autorhythmic, overriding the slower signal arriving from the SA node. Ventricular fibrillation can cause the ventricles to contract as many as 300 times per minute, a rate too fast to effectively move blood through the circulatory system. Rapid intervention is required with this condition to prevent complete heart failure and death. The heart can be shocked out of fibrillation with a device called a defibrillator. For certain cardiac patients, there are internal versions of defibrillators, called implantable cardioverter defibrillators, or ICDs, that return the heart to its normal rhythm when fibrillation occurs.

HEART SOUNDS

By using a stethoscope, two major heart sounds can be heard during each cardiac cycle . These sounds are associated with the closing of the heart valves. (There is a third type of sound that is occasionally heard in children only.) The first heart sound occurs when the AV valves between the atria and ventricles close at the start of ventricular systole (see Figure 6.4, bottom). This sound tends to be louder than the second sound. The second major heart sound occurs at the end of ventricular systole when the semilunar valves close.

ICDs are intended only for those patients with particularly dangerous heart irregularities, also known as **arrhythmias**. Pacemakers, implanted under the skin in or near the chest, are used to control the more common arrhythmias, meaning those heart rhythms that are too fast, too slow, or otherwise irregular. All arrhythmias can affect the ability of the heart to pump blood properly, thereby limiting a person's level of physical activity. Pacemakers help such patients, who are often elderly or have heart disease, to lead more active lifestyles.

Most pacemakers are permanently implanted and consist of an electrical generator that is computerized, a battery pack, and electrodes and wires that deliver the electrical discharges to the heart while monitoring the heart's rhythm. Certain pacemakers can also monitor the level of the patient's activity and respond appropriately. The computer also records the electrical activity of the heart, allowing the doctor to examine how the pacemaker and heart are functioning and to make adjustments to the program if needed. There are a variety of pacemakers available; all of them require minor surgery for implantation. The batteries that power the pacemakers can last from 5 to 15 years, and surgery is also required to replace them when they begin to run down.

MEASURES OF HEART FUNCTION

Cardiac output, or **CO**, is the volume of blood ejected by each ventricle in one minute. It indicates the level of efficiency of the heart as a pump. Cardiac output is the product of the heart rate (HR) times the **stroke volume (SV)**. The stroke volume is the volume of blood pumped out by a ventricle with each beat. For example, if the heart rate is 65 beats per minute (bpm) and the stroke volume is 75 milliliters per beat, then cardiac output will equal 4,875 milliliters per minute (mL/min), or about 4.9 liters per minute (L/min).

The stroke volume can be calculated by subtracting the volume of blood at the end of ventricular systole (the *end-systolic volume*, or *ESV*) from the volume present at the start of the contraction phase (the *end-diastolic volume*, or *EDV*). Note in Figure 6.4 that the volume of blood in the ventricle starts to increase as the ventricle refills with blood with the onset of ventricular diastole.

In a resting individual, at the start of a new cardiac cycle, there is about 60 mL of blood remaining from the previous cycle; this is the end-systolic volume. Another 30 mL is added passively as blood returns to the atria and flows through the open AV valves into the ventricles. Atrial systole adds another 40 mL to the volume in the ventricles, for a total of 130 mL, the end-diastolic volume. Once the stroke volume of 70 mL is ejected during ventricular systole, there is 60 mL left, the end-systolic volume, which is the starting point.

Adjustments to both stroke volume and heart rate are made to maintain an adequate supply of blood to the tissues. With heavy exercise, for example, cardiac output can increase from roughly 5 L/min to 18 to 40 L/min, depending on an individual's level of fitness. This volume is impressive; consider lining up 9 to 20 2-liter bottles of soda in a row to form a picture of how hard the heart is working. This increase is achieved primarily through an increase in the heart rate and also in the stroke volume.

Any changes in the EDV and/or the ESV of the ventricle will affect the stroke volume. (Recall that the stroke volume = EDV – ESV.) The EDV is affected by the time available for filling of the ventricle. As the heart rate speeds up, there is less time between contractions for blood to fill the ventricles. The EDV is also dependent on the rate of return of blood to the heart by the venous system, known as **venous return**. If the ESV remains unchanged, then any decrease in EDV will cause the SV to decrease, while an increase in EDV will result in an increased SV.

At rest, the stroke volume is less than 55% of the EDV, a percentage called the *ejection fraction*. The remaining blood, about 60 mL, is the ESV. With strenuous exercise in trained athletes, the ejection fraction can be increased to as much as 90% of the EDV, significantly reducing the ESV. The ejection fraction is an important measure of cardiac function.

It should be noted that the stroke volumes for the right and left ventricles are the same (that is, they both eject the same volume of blood with every contraction of the heart). A mismatch between the stroke volumes can lead to severe health problems, including a condition known as **congestive heart failure**. If, for example, left heart function is reduced and leads to a reduction in stroke volume, blood backs up in the lungs, forcing fluid into the interstitium and making it very difficult to breathe. Similarly, right heart failure leads to systemic edema, the accumulation of fluid in the systemic interstitium, as blood backs up in the systemic circuit.

CONNECTIONS

The heart generates its own rhythm for contraction. Pacemaker cells in the sinoatrial (SA) node relay a signal through the

(continues on page 76)

(continued from page 75)

conducting system of the heart. Other structures in this conducting system help to coordinate the contractions that this signal elicits. For example, the AV node delays transmission of the signal to the ventricles, allowing time for atrial contraction and ventricular filling.

The cardiac cycle represents the changes in pressure and volume that accompany atrial and ventricular diastole and systole. While the volume of blood ejected by the right and left ventricles (the stroke volume) is identical, the pressures generated by the two ventricles differ greatly. The left ventricle must pump its stroke volume against the much higher pressure of the systemic circuit. Pumping blood against the lower pressure within the pulmonary circuit requires less work by the right ventricle.

Cardiac output is an important measure of heart function and is determined by multiplying the heart rate times the stroke volume. Hence, changes in cardiac output can be achieved through alterations in either of these two variables. Chapter 8 provides two examples of how cardiac output is affected by challenges to circulation, in the forms of hemorrhage and exercise.

7

Control of Blood Pressure and Distribution

BLOOD PRESSURE PLAYS AN IMPORTANT ROLE IN THE PROPER functioning of the circulatory system. Blood only moves when it is under pressure. The heart generates this pressure, which drives blood through the entire system of blood vessels to every part of the body. When doctors or nurses check someone's blood pressure, they gain valuable information about how well the patient's circulatory system is working: Is the blood pressure normal? Is it too high or too low? The search for the answers to these questions starts with the two numbers that are recorded after the blood pressure cuff is wrapped around the arm and inflated. But what exactly do these numbers mean? And what is meant by "too high" or "too low"?

BLOOD PRESSURE

Blood flow (and, therefore, blood pressure) within all arteries occurs in waves, or pulses, that are synchronized with the cardiac cycle. Blood pressure is highest during ventricular systole, when blood is being forced into the arteries. Arterial blood pressure is lowest during ventricular diastole, when the heart is refilling with blood. These two pressures together represent a blood pressure measurement, often stated as the higher, or systolic, pressure "over" the lower, or diastolic, pressure. Systolic pressure is typically 120 mm Hg or less in a healthy person, while diastolic pressure is usually 80 mm Hg or less. A blood pressure recording of 110 over 70 mm Hg would be an example of a healthy blood pressure reading for most adults.

Measuring the blood pressure by using a **blood pressure cuff** makes use of the principles of Boyle's law, which describes the relationship between pressure and volume. The cuff is inflated to a pressure well above that of the higher systolic pressure, blocking flow within the brachial artery of the arm. As the pressure in the cuff is slowly released, blood begins to squirt through the vessel during ventricular systole, creating a sound. It is at this point that the pressure in the cuff equals the systolic pressure. As cuff pressure is reduced further, the sound will disappear once the brachial artery is fully open so that blood flow is no longer interrupted at any point in the cardiac cycle. The pressure at which the sounds disappear represents the diastolic pressure.

FACTORS AFFECTING BLOOD PRESSURE

As you learned in Chapter 6, the heart generates the pressure that moves blood through its circuits. One of the factors that affects blood pressure is heart function, or cardiac output. Cardiac output is a measure of the efficiency of the heart and indicates how much blood volume the heart is pumping per unit of time, typically in millimeters per minute. If either stroke volume or heart rate increases, then cardiac output increases. When cardiac output increases, blood pressure also rises. Conversely, if either stroke volume or heart rate decreases, blood pressure decreases as well.

Other factors that affect blood pressure include blood volume, total peripheral resistance, and blood viscosity. As the volume of blood within the circulatory system increases, blood pressure increases. Loss of blood from a major injury causes blood pressure to drop. In such a case, the immediate replacement of the lost blood with a blood transfusion can help to restore blood pressure. Loss of blood pressure can mean insufficient blood flow to the body's tissues, and the subsequent lack of oxygen can cause permanent damage or death.

Total peripheral resistance, or *TPR*, is a measure of the degree of resistance to blood flow within the blood vessels and is related to the vessel diameter, among other factors. Arterioles are considered to be the resistance vessels of the circulatory system. When these vessels constrict, their diameters decrease, generating more friction between the flowing blood and the vessel walls and increasing TPR, or the resistance to the flow of blood. Conversely, when these vessels dilate, or open up, their diameters increase, reducing the amount of friction between blood and the vessel walls and decreasing the TPR. Blood pressure must exceed this resistance for the flow to continue. For this reason, with an increase in peripheral resistance, the blood pressure increases. Blood pressure drops in response to vasodilation and reduced peripheral resistance. While the relationship between blood vessel diameter and resistance to blood flow holds true for all blood vessels, it is the arterioles that exert the greatest effect on blood pressure.

Blood is primarily water, but it also contains cells and proteins (see Chapter 3). The viscosity of blood is a measure of its resistance to flow. The higher the viscosity of the blood, the greater its resistance to flow and the more energy or pressure is required to propel it through the circulatory system. Usually, the viscosity of blood remains constant, but there are conditions that can cause viscosity to increase, leading to an increase in blood pressure. Likewise, a decrease in viscosity will lead to a decrease in blood pressure.

The important relationship between cardiac output, TPR, and blood pressure (meaning arterial blood pressure) can be expressed in the formula:

Blood pressure = Cardiac output x Total peripheral resistance

Using this formula, it is possible to predict how a change in cardiac output or peripheral resistance will affect blood pressure.

THE BAROMETER FOR BLOOD PRESSURE DROPS

In 2003, the definition of healthy blood pressure changed for adults 18 years and older. For years, a systolic pressure of 120 mm Hg with a diastolic pressure of 80 mm Hg was considered to be healthy. The National Heart, Lung, and Blood Institute has now categorized systolic pressures of 120 to 149 mm Hg and diastolic pressures of 80 to 90 mm Hg as "prehypertension," meaning an individual with these values is at risk for developing hypertension, or high blood pressure. This change means that 45 million previously healthy individuals must now make some lifestyle changes, such as losing weight and exercising, to reduce their blood pressure. Table 7.1 lists the revised guidelines for blood pressure recordings and includes recommended treatments for two stages of hypertension. The new classifications are a result of recent scientific studies demonstrating that an increased risk of heart disease occurs with blood pressures lower than previously believed.

What causes high blood pressure? The most common causes include vasoconstriction or narrowing of the arteries (which increases TPR), a greater than normal volume of blood (which can result from lots of salt in the diet), or an increase in heart rate or stroke volume due to more forceful contractions than normal. Any of these conditions will cause increased pressure against the walls of the arteries.

One-third of Americans with hypertension are undiagnosed and completely unaware they have this dangerous condition. Hypertension places an individual at increased risk for heart attacks, strokes, kidney failure, and heart failure, all potentially lethal conditions. For this reason, hypertension is called the "silent killer"

BLOOD PRESSURES THROUGHOUT THE CIRCULATORY SYSTEM

The measurement of blood pressure indicates the *arterial* blood pressure. Blood pressure is the force that moves blood continuously through the circulatory system. Blood will only

because individuals may not know they have the disease until after they suffer serious damage.

Those classified with prehypertension are more likely to develop hypertension and heart disease and need to take action. For every 20-point rise in systolic pressure above 115 mm Hg or 10-point rise in diastolic pressure above 75 mm Hg, the risk for heart disease doubles. Medication is not recommended for prehypertension. Instead, officials recommend that these individuals lose weight if they are overweight, avoid excess salt, stay physically active, stop smoking, and limit their alcohol consumption. Because blood pressure values typically rise with age as arteries become more rigid and lose their elasticity, older Americans need to be more vigilant in following these recommendations.

About 50 million Americans have been diagnosed with hypertension, but officials estimate that two-thirds of these patients do not have their high blood pressure under control. The new guidelines also make recommendations for treatment. These recommendations differ based on the severity of the hypertension, defined as Stage I or II, and whether other conditions exist or not. Health officials found that one of the most effective medications for hypertension, a class of drugs known as diuretics, is also one of the cheapest to prescribe.

Diuretics, like the drug furosemide (known as Lasix), act on the kidneys to increase urine volume, thereby reducing blood volume and blood pressure. Low-salt diets are likewise recommended for reducing and preventing hypertension. Eating salt causes thirst and the drinking of fluids, thereby expanding blood volume and raising blood pressure until the kidneys have time to correct the volume overload.

TABLE 7.1 NEW GUIDELINES FOR BLOOD PRESSURE

PRESSURE (mm Hg)	NORMAL	PRE-HYPERTENTION	STAGE I HYPERTENTION	STAGE II HYPERTENTION
Systolic	Less than 120	120–139	140–159	More than 160
Diastolic	Less than 80	80–89	90–99	More than 100
DRUG TREATMENT				
Only condition	None	None	Diuretics; occasionally other drugs	Two-drug combo; typically one is a diurectic
Other conditions*	None	Treat other diseases	Multiple medications	Multiple medications

* Treatments for hypertension with other conditions are only approved for patients 18 and older.

move in the presence of a pressure difference and will always flow from a region of higher pressure to a region of lower pressure. Blood pressure decreases with increased distance from the left ventricle. Pressures are highest in the arteries and decrease as blood moves to the venous side of the system. This pressure difference ensures that blood moves in only one direction, from the arterial to the venous side and back to the heart.

As you learned in Chapter 5, arteries and veins have, on average, much larger diameters than capillaries. However, the total cross-sectional area of the capillaries (the number of vessels and their diameters) is much greater than that of either the arteries or veins.

Blood flows at a faster rate through the larger arteries where pressure is high and the resistance is low. In contrast, after the vessels have branched numerous times, the rate of blood flow as it approaches the capillaries slows significantly. Since the capillaries are the site of exchange of materials between the blood and the tissues, the slower rate of blood flow allows adequate time for **capillary exchange** to occur.

CAPILLARY EXCHANGE

To accommodate capillary exchange, the walls of the capillaries are extremely thin, consisting of a single layer of endothelial cells with a basement membrane. Here, materials are exchanged between the blood and the tissues. Water, ions, glucose, amino acids, oxygen, carbon dioxide, and the waste product urea pass through the endothelial cell junctions according to their concentration gradients. Larger molecules, blood proteins, and cells are too large to move through the cell junctions and are, therefore, retained within the capillaries.

In addition to diffusion, other processes are involved in the movement of materials across the capillary wall. The pressure differences between the blood and the interstitial fluid surrounding the tissue cells promote the movement of fluid out of the blood through the endothelial cell junctions into the tissues, a process known as **filtration**. Because blood pressure decreases along the length of the capillary, the rate of filtration decreases as well. Filtration is highest at the arterial end of the capillary and lowest at the venous end.

Another process, **reabsorption**, counteracts filtration. In reabsorption, some of the interstitial fluid moves back into the capillary. As water and dissolved substances (or solutes) move via diffusion and filtration from the blood into the interstitial fluid, the remaining solutes, and particularly the proteins, increase in concentration. Any excess fluid retained within the interstitial fluid will be picked up by the lymph vessels of the lymphatic system and returned into circulation at a point near the heart.

In addition to the need for oxygen and nutrients like glucose, cells also need water. Water moves into and out of the tissues by diffusion. In the diffusion of water, known as **osmosis**, water moves across membranes from a region of lower solute concentration (higher water concentration) to one of higher solute concentration (lower water concentration).

To summarize, filtration forces water and solutes out of the capillaries and into the interstitial fluid, while reabsorption promotes the movement of water and solutes from the interstitial fluid back into the capillaries. The balance of these two opposing forces changes along the length of the capillary. In the initial, arterial portion of the capillary, the rate of filtration exceeds the rate of reabsorption. However, toward the venous end of the capillary, the rate of reabsorption is greater than the rate of filtration.

Any condition that affects the blood pressure, the interstitial pressure, or the osmotic pressure of the blood can alter the dynamic balance between the forces of filtration and reabsorption. For example, with **kwashiorkor**, a protein-deficiency disease, the osmotic pressure of the blood is low because of a lack of blood proteins. As a result, the rate of reabsorption by the capillaries is greatly reduced and unable to effectively counteract filtration. Interstitial fluid accumulates in the tissues, leading to a condition known as *edema* and the appearance of a swollen belly.

If blood pressure decreases, perhaps in response to a **hemorrhage** (heavy bleeding), capillary filtration will be reduced. In this case, reabsorption will dominate and interstitial fluid will move into the blood. In this way, interstitial fluid acts as a reserve of fluid for replacing blood when blood volume drops.

VENOUS RETURN

Venous pressure is an important determinant of venous return (the amount of blood that is returned to the heart during circulation) and of cardiac output. The rate of flow in the veins increases as blood flows from the smaller diameter venules and veins to larger veins where the diameters are greater and the resistance to flow is lower.

When the body is in a standing position, blood must overcome gravity to return from the region below the heart. How does venous return take place in someone standing up, considering the low pressure gradients found in the venous system and the pull of gravity? As described previously, contractions of the skeletal muscles, also known as the **skeletal muscle pump**, can compress the veins and help squeeze the blood past the one-way valves that prevent backflow. Venous return is further aided by what is called the **respiratory pump**.

When the chest cavity expands during inhalation, the pressure within that cavity is decreased. This action lowers the pressures in the largest vessels that return blood to the heart, which thereby creates a more favorable pressure gradient for the blood to reach the heart. In addition, neural input can help with venous return by stimulating constriction of the veins.

REGULATION OF CIRCULATORY FUNCTION

One of the primary functions of the circulatory system is to deliver oxygen-rich blood to the body's tissues. The oxygen is used by cells to make ATP, an energy-storage compound, in a process called *cellular respiration*. Carbon dioxide is a waste product of cellular respiration, and it must be removed from the body efficiently or it will adversely affect acid-base balance. The circulatory system must also remove harmful nitrogenous waste products like urea.

Changes in cardiac output, peripheral resistance, and blood pressure play a role in how the circulatory system adjusts to ensure that the oxygen demands of the tissues are matched by an adequate supply of oxygen-rich blood. To ensure that the responses of the circulatory system are made in a coordinated and appropriate manner, there are multiple levels of control and feedback.

Some control occurs on a local level. For example, if a particular tissue is not obtaining an adequate supply of blood, it produces signals that result in an increased blood flow that focuses on that particular region. This form of control is called **autoregulation**. This increase in local flow is achieved through the release of *vasodilators*. Vasodilators, such as carbon dioxide and lactic acid, act locally to dilate the precapillary sphincters in nearby capillary beds and thus enhance blood flow only to the specific region that is affected.

There are other substances that can cause the precapillary sphincters to constrict and cut off the blood flow to the affected capillary beds. Vasoconstricting substances are most often released when the wall of a blood vessel is damaged. Injured cells release a vasoconstrictor called histamine, while activated platelets adhering to the damaged tissue release other vasoconstrictors and thereby reduce blood loss at the site of injury.

In addition to local control, there is neural control of circulatory function. In cases where blood flow is being diverted to one tissue to meet its increased oxygen demand, it is essential that this action does not deprive another important tissue of its blood flow. To keep this from happening, the nervous system acts to regulate both cardiac output and total peripheral resistance. These cardiovascular centers, located within the medulla oblongata of the brainstem, are groups of neurons that regulate these two important variables. These neurons belong to two different systems: the sympathetic and the parasympathetic nervous systems. In general, these systems have opposite effects on the target tissue.

Another method of regulation is through **baroreceptors**, pressure receptors that respond to stretch. They are located in the walls of the carotid arteries and the aortic arch and are able to sense changes in blood pressure (Figure 7.1). A decrease in the firing rate of the baroreceptors signals a drop

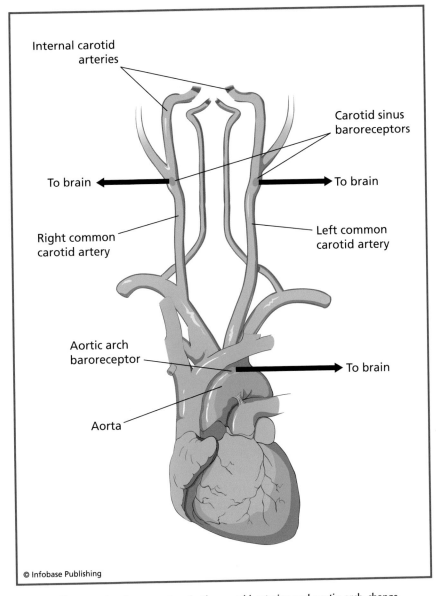

Figure 7.1   Baroreceptors in the carotid arteries and aortic arch change their rate of firing in response to changes in blood pressure. This information is relayed to the cardiovascular center located in the medulla oblongata of the brain stem.

BLOOD PRESSURE IN OUTER SPACE

After more than 30 years of space travel, scientists have learned that life in space affects almost every body system. In low-gravity conditions, or microgravity, astronauts lose muscle mass in their legs; they also lose bone mass due to demineralization. The immune system does not work normally in space, apparently because the white blood cells do not function efficiently. Space travel also has adverse effects on other aspects of the human circulatory system in addition to the white blood cells.

Without gravity, body fluids, including blood, shift away from the lower body into the upper body, causing blood to pool in the chest and head (Figure 7.2). This fluid shift affects the heart, which becomes enlarged in order to deal with the excess blood flow. Over time, the fluid shift is perceived by the body to be excess volume, causing responses that significantly reduce the blood volume.

Space physiologists who have observed these changes have two basic questions: First, how does this blood volume shift and eventual blood volume reduction affect an astronaut's health and ability to carry out assigned tasks? Second, are these effects reversible upon return to Earth or are there long-term consequences of space travel on an astronaut's health?

When someone stands up quickly, gravity draws the blood to the large veins in the legs and abdomen and away from the upper body and brain. When someone stands up too quickly, this causes blood pressure to drop and the person may feel light headed. Usually, however, the circulatory system makes immediate adjustments in blood pressure to restore flow to the upper body and counteract the effects of gravity. However, astronauts face a greater challenge: Of those who spend more than two weeks in space, 20% of them are unable to stand up without getting dizzy, a condition known as *orthostatic intolerance.* According to a study conducted by the National Aeronautics and Space Administration (NASA), the longer an astronaut remains in space, the greater the risk of orthostatic intolerance.

Space physiologists have also noted that astronauts have an increased incidence of arrhythmias in space. The direct cause of this response is unknown. Astronauts also suffer from anemia, which is

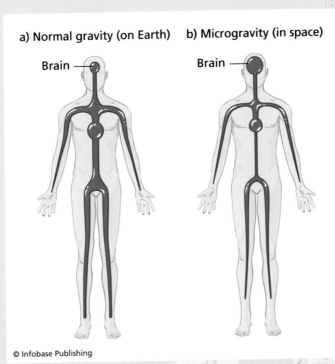

a) Normal gravity (on Earth)   b) Microgravity (in space)

Brain   Brain

© Infobase Publishing

Figure 7.2   In the microgravity of space, body fluids, including blood, shift to the upper regions of the body, eventually leading to a reduction in blood volume. Upon return to Earth's gravitational field, the majority of the blood volume shifts back into the lower body, and because the volume is reduced, blood pressure drops too low. Under such circumstances, standing may lead to dizziness.

a reduced number of circulating red blood cells. The space-related anemia appears to be due to a diminished production of new red blood cells rather than an increase in the destruction of red blood cells. Scientists studying space-related anemia use prolonged bed rest on Earth, which also results in anemia, as a model for their investigations.

Another factor affected by the circulatory system's response to microgravity is the effectiveness of medical drugs. Many of the

(continues on page 90)

(continued from page 89)
drugs that are delivered to their action sites by the circulatory system do not appear to work as well in space as they do on Earth. Space physiologists are not sure whether this is the result of a delivery problem due to the circulatory adjustments to space or due to an increase in the rate of drug elimination by the liver and kidney, two organs that become enlarged under zero-gravity conditions.

It can take astronauts months, or even years, to recover from some of the changes described above after they have returned to Earth. With plans for longer and longer periods of human habitation on space stations under way, it is clear that more research is needed on the short- and long-term physiological effects of space travel.

in blood pressure to the medullary cardiovascular center in the brain. This center also receives input from **chemoreceptors** in the aortic arch and carotid arteries. The chemoreceptors alert the center if, for example, carbon dioxide levels in the blood become elevated or oxygen levels drop. In either case, the response to elevated blood carbon dioxide levels or a drop in blood pressure is the same, since both variables signal that blood flow to the tissues is compromised.

Increased output from sympathetic nerves to the sinoatrial node of the heart causes the heart rate to increase. Stroke volume is enhanced because of an increase in *contractility* of the heart muscle, or its ability to contract, again in response to a sympathetic discharge from the cardioregulatory center in the medulla. Sympathetic discharge from the center to the veins results in vasoconstriction and enhanced venous return to support the increase in cardiac output. Vasoconstriction in the systemic arterioles is also mediated by sympathetic outflow from the center, raising the total peripheral resistance.

In addition to local and neural control, changes in circulatory function can also be initiated by certain hormones. The heart and blood vessels can respond directly to circulating hormones through the presence of hormone receptors in these tissues. Thyroid hormone, for example, increases the heart rate. Likewise, other circulating chemicals in the blood can alter circulatory function. Stimulants, such as caffeine and nicotine, elevate the heart rate by enhancing the impact of neurotransmitters, such as epinephrine and norepinephrine, that are released by the sympathetic system.

CONNECTIONS

Blood pressure represents the critical force that powers the circulation of blood through the tissues. Blood pressure is affected by a variety of factors including cardiac output (through changes in stroke volume and/or heart rate), blood volume, blood viscosity, and total peripheral resistance.

Blood pressure and the rate of blood flow vary throughout the circulatory system. Blood pressures and flow rates are high in the arteries. Flow rates are particularly low in the capillaries. There is a great increase in the resistance to flow in these vessels because of their large number and small diameter. The slower flow allows adequate time for the process of capillary exchange.

There are a variety of controls on circulatory function. Local control ensures that individual tissues can meet their oxygen needs by adjusting their blood supply. However, the nervous system plays the key regulatory role in circulatory function through the coordination of blood flow to the various tissues. Baroreceptors provide information about blood pressure to the cardiovascular center in the medulla, which acts to make the appropriate adjustments through changes in sympathetic and parasympathetic output to the heart and blood vessels.

8

Circulatory Responses to Hemorrhage and Exercise

KNOWING HOW THE CIRCULATORY SYSTEM FUNCTIONS normally is important for learning how the system operates under other conditions, such as in the period following an injury or during exercise. One of the best ways to underscore how the circulatory system functions is to challenge that system to adapt to a new physiological situation. This chapter will first examine how the human body attempts to counteract the deleterious effects of severe hemorrhage, or major blood loss, before investigating how the circulatory system reponds to exercise.

CIRCULATORY RESPONSES TO HEMORRHAGE

The term *hemorrhage* is used to describe a significant loss of blood volume, either externally or internally. Internal bleeding is often difficult to detect, but still requires immediate attention. Once a significant volume of blood is lost from circulation, the effects can be truly life threatening as it gets harder and harder to maintain blood pressure and therefore blood flow to the tissues.

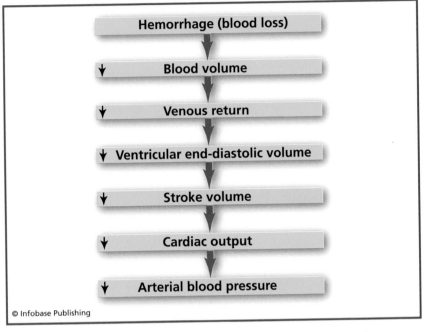

Figure 8.1 Factors leading to a drop in blood pressure with hemorrhage. The loss of blood volume leads to a decrease in venous pressure and a reduction in the return of blood to the heart. A reduction in venous return causes a decrease in cardiac output and arterial blood pressure.

The loss of blood causes a decrease in venous return to the heart and subsequently a decrease in stroke volume, which is the amount of blood pumped by the heart with each contraction. As a result, cardiac output is reduced. A decrease in cardiac output causes a decrease in blood pressure (Figure 8.1). Blood pressure, the force that moves blood throughout the circulatory system, must be restored to a level that allows adequate blood flow to the tissues so they do not suffer irreversible damage from oxygen starvation.

The drop in blood pressure is sensed by the baroreceptors, which decrease their rate of firing as blood pressure drops. Changes in the firing rate of the baroreceptors are sensed by the cardiovascular center of the medulla oblongata of the brainstem, and a suite of homeostatic, or stabilizing, mechanisms is set in motion to help return blood pressure level to normal.

Using the formula described earlier, it is possible to predict how the body will respond to counteract the drop in blood pressure that accompanies hemorrhage. Recall that Blood pressure = Cardiac output x Total peripheral resistance. Therefore, to increase blood pressure, the mechanisms that promote an increase in cardiac output and/or total peripheral resistance would be called into action. Because Cardiac output = Heart rate x Stroke volume, increasing the heart rate and/or stroke volume should also help restore adequate blood pressure.

When the decreased firing rate of the baroreceptors is sensed by the cardiovascular center of the medulla, it causes an increase in sympathetic stimulation to the sinoatrial (SA) node in the right atrium, and the heart rate increases (Figure 8.2). The heart attempts to maintain stroke volume increases by generating more forceful ventricular contractions. In summary, to compensate for blood loss, the body attempts to maintain cardiac output through adjustments to stroke volume and heart rate.

The cardiovascular center of the medulla also increases its sympathetic output to certain blood vessels. Recall that veins are called capacitance vessels because at any one time they contain a large percentage of the circulating blood volume. Increased sympathetic stimulation to the veins results in vasoconstriction, forcing some of the blood volume from the veins into the rest of the circulatory system. This action increases venous return to the heart, helping to maintain stroke volume via a different mechanism. Keeping a hemorrhaging individual lying down also aids venous return to the heart because it reduces gravitational pull on the blood returning from the lower body regions.

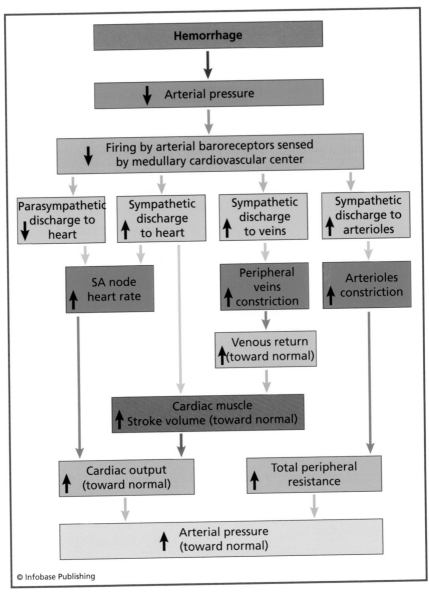

Figure 8.2   This diagram illustrates the response of the baroreceptors and cardiovascular centers to a decrease in blood pressure. Increased sympathetic discharge to the heart, veins, and arterioles triggers changes that help return blood pressure toward the normal range. A "down" arrow in a box indicates a decrease in an activity, while an "up" arrow indicates an increase.

Finally, sympathetic output from the cardiovascular center also acts directly on the arterioles, which are also called resistance vessels. Recall that small changes in the diameter of these vessels can have a huge impact on blood pressure. In this case, increased sympathetic discharge induces vasoconstriction of the arterioles, causing total peripheral resistance to rise, which, up to a point, will help to maintain blood pressure and flow. Remember, no pressure equals no flow.

To summarize, a drop in blood pressure results in increased sympathetic discharge from the medullary cardiovascular center to the SA node, the cardiac muscle, the veins, and the arterioles. The net result is an increased cardiac output and increased total peripheral resistance, leading to an increase in blood pressure.

Hormonal responses also play a role. Increased levels of angiotensin II and antidiuretic hormones promote vasoconstriction and elevate total peripheral resistance. Both hormones also promote restoration of blood volume as they induce a powerful sense of thirst.

CIRCULATORY RESPONSES TO EXERCISE

To meet the increased oxygen needs of active tissues during exercise, cardiac output must increase. Output can increase from a resting rate of 5 liters per minute to a value as high as 40 liters per minute in athletes. The increase in cardiac output is accomplished primarily through an increase in heart rate. Stroke volume also increases, though to a lesser degree.

The distribution of blood flow changes as a person goes from the resting to the active state. Increased flow to the exercising muscles, the skin, and the heart is achieved through vasodilation of the arterioles and opening of the precapillary sphincters to the capillary beds in those organs (Figure 8.3). The exercising muscles and heart require more oxygen for their increased activity levels, and the flow to the skin helps to unload excess body heat. At the same time, blood flow to the digestive system and kidneys is reduced

	Rest (ml/min)	Strenuous Exercise (ml/min)
Brain	650 (13%)	750 (4%)
Heart	215 (4%)	750 (4%)
Skeletal muscle	1,030 (20%)	12,500 (73%)
Skin	430 (9%)	1,900 (11%)
Kidney	950 (20%)	600 (3%)
Abdominal organs	1,200 (24%)	600 (3%)
Other	525 (10%)	400 (2%)
Total	5,000	17,500

Figure 8.3 The distribution of blood flow changes as a person goes from a resting to a strenuously active state. There is increased flow to the heart, active skeletal muscles, and skin (to facilitate heat loss), while blood flow to the abdominal organs and kidneys is decreased. (Percentages represent total blood flow.)

because the nervous system stimulates vasoconstriction in these tissues.

Overall, blood pressure increases by a small amount with exercise. Although cardiac output increases, total peripheral resistance drops due to widespread vasodilation. In this way, the drop in total peripheral resistance mostly offsets the rise in cardiac output; hence, blood pressure increases only a small degree.

Venous return, or the return of blood to the heart, must also increase to maintain a high cardiac output. Increased venous return with exercise is aided by several mechanisms, including increased sympathetic output to the veins, which stimulates vasoconstriction in those vessels. As with hemorrhage, this response helps to reduce the volume of blood carried by the veins, forcing that volume toward the heart. In addition, the skeletal muscle and respiratory pumps are more active with exercise, increasing venous return and cardiac output.

The nervous system plays a key role in the circulatory responses to exercise. In fact, the mere anticipation of exercise can induce certain circulatory responses before an individual actually begins to exercise. For example, increased sympathetic and decreased parasympathetic input to the heart from the medullary cardiovascular center enhances cardiac output prior to exercise. With exercise, increased sympathetic output to the arterioles lowers total peripheral resistance, and increased sympathetic output to the veins increases venous return with exercise.

Local mechanisms play a role as well. As activity increases, the partial pressure of oxygen decreases the exercising tissue and the partial pressure of carbon dioxide and the acidity levels increase. These changes signal a need for increased blood flow to these regions. Vasodilation of the blood vessels in these tissues allows for increased flow to meet the change in oxygen demand. In addition, the Bohr effect enhances the unloading of oxygen from hemoglobin circulating through these tissues. Figure 8.4 summarizes many of the short-term changes in circulatory function that accompany exercise.

Years of physical exercise can lead to long-term changes in circulatory function. Training increases an individual's maximum cardiac output, the factor which most often limits the ability of the body to meet the increased oxygen demands required to meet an increase in workload. Long-term physical training has a significant impact on stroke volume. An increased stroke volume is achieved through enhanced

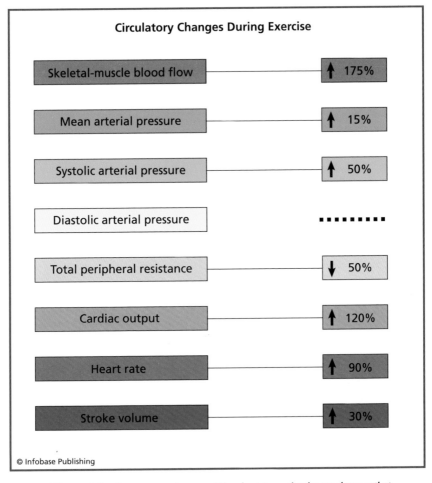

Figure 8.4   A summary of some of the short-term circulatory changes that occur with exercise. Total peripheral resistance decreases with exercise due to vasodilation. Blood pressure, heart rate, cardiac output, and stroke volume all increase, helping to increase blood flow to the active skeletal muscles.

pumping ability of the heart. The ventricular walls thicken, contract more forcibly, and eject more blood with each heart beat. As a consequence, the degree to which the heart rate is elevated for a given workload is reduced in trained athletes (Figure 8.5).

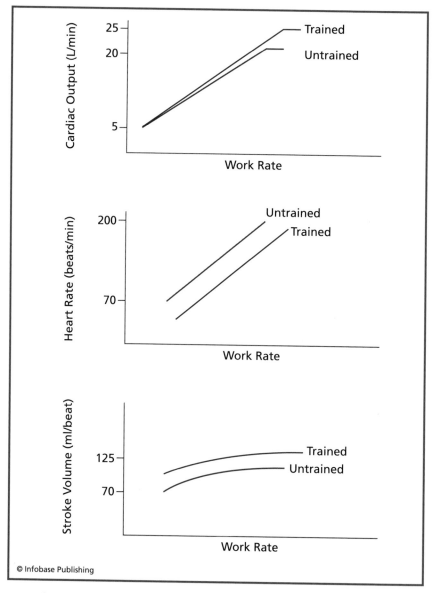

Figure 8.5 Changes in heart function accompany extensive physical training. With training, the maximum cardiac output increases. The heart does not strain as hard to pump blood to the body, so heart rate is decreased. With training, the stroke volume is increased, reducing the demand on heart rate.

In addition, an increase in the number of mitochondria as well as the enzymes of cellular respiration occurs within the skeletal muscles involved in training. As a consequence, these muscles use oxygen and fuel more efficiently, improving their endurance.

CONNECTIONS

Examining how the human circulatory system adjusts to challenges helps us to understand better how the system works. With hemorrhage, the loss of blood volume leads to a decrease in blood pressure that must be returned to normal to prevent tissue damage and death. Massive sympathetic output by the cardiovascular center of the medulla triggers homeostatic mechanisms that contribute to reversing the decrease in blood pressure. Direct effects on the SA node and cardiac muscle enhance cardiac output. Vasoconstriction of the veins increases venous return, while vasoconstriction of the systemic arterioles raises the total peripheral resistance.

Short-term circulatory responses to exercise are primarily achieved through the actions of the cardiovascular center as well, although local control plays a role in ensuring that the more active tissues receive an adequate blood supply. The increase in cardiac output seen with exercise is primarily accomplished through an increase in heart rate. With long-term physical training, however, stroke volume is also enhanced.

Exercise also alters the distribution of blood flow to organs. It increases blood flow to the active tissues, the heart, and skin while reducing flow to the kidneys and organs of the digestive system. It also enhances venous return through the increased activity of the skeletal muscle and respiratory pumps and vasoconstriction in the veins. Blood pressure is only slightly elevated with exercise because the increase in cardiac output is offset by a drop in total peripheral resistance due to widespread vasodilation.

Appendix: Conversion Chart

Unit (metric)	Metric to English	English to Metric
LENGTH		
Kilometer km	1 km 0.62 mile (mi)	1 mile (mi) 1.609 km
Meter m	1 m 3.28 feet (ft)	1 foot (ft) 0.305 m
Centimeter cm	1 cm 0.394 inches (in)	1 inch (in) 2.54 cm
Millimeter mm	1 mm 0.039 inches (in)	1 inch (in) 25.4 mm
Micrometer μm	1-millionth meter	
WEIGHT (MASS)		
Kilogram kg	1 kg 2.2 pounds (lbs)	1 pound (lbs) 0.454 kg
Gram g	1 g 0.035 ounces (oz)	1 ounce (oz) 28.35 g
Milligram mg	1 mg 0.000035 ounces (oz)	
Microgram μg	1-millionth gram	
VOLUME		
Liter L	1 L 1.06 quarts	1 gallon (gal) 3.785 L
		1 quart (qt) 0.94 L
		1 pint (pt) 0.47 L
Milliliter mL or cc	1 mL 0.034 fluid ounce (fl oz)	1 fluid ounce (fl oz) 29.57 mL
Microliter μL	1-millionth liter	
TEMPERATURE		
	$°F = 9/5°C + 32$	$°C = 5/9 (°F - 32)$

Glossary

Adenosine triphosphate (ATP)   An energy storage compound produced by cellular respiration.

Affinity   Ability of a molecule to bind a substrate.

Albumins   A class of blood plasma proteins.

Anemia   Low red blood cell count.

Angina   Any disease characterized by spasmodic suffocative attacks—for example, angina pectoris, a paroxysmal thoracic pain with feeling of suffocation.

Angioplasty   Also called percutaneous transluminal coronary angioplasty (PTCA). Dilation of a plaque-lined artery to increase blood flow by insertion of catheter with deflated balloon at its tip into narrowed artery. Once inserted, the balloon is inflated, compressing the plaque and enlarging the inner diameter of the blood vessel.

Antibodies   Proteins produced by white blood cells that fight foreign invaders, such as bacteria and viruses.

Antigen   Substance that, when introduced into the body, causes formation of antibodies against it.

Aortic semilunar valve   Heart valve that separates the left ventricle from the ascending aorta.

Arrhythmia   Abnormal heartbeat.

Arteries   Muscular blood vessels that carry blood away from the heart.

Arterioles   Small muscular blood vessels that deliver blood to the capillaries.

Ascending aorta   The initial portion of the aortic arch into which blood is forced by the left ventricle.

Atherosclerosis   A condition in which fatty plaques form on the walls of arteries; also known as hardening of the arteries.

Atria   Plural of atrium. *See* atrium.

Antrioventricular bundle   Nerve fibers that carry impulses from the AV node to the ventricles; they branch to form Purkinje fibers.

Atrioventricular (AV) node   Small mass of special cardiac muscle tissue located in the right atrium along the lower part of the interatrial septum.

Atrioventricular valves   Flaps of tissue that separate the atria from the ventricles; also known as AV valves.

Atrium   One of the two upper chambers of the heart that receive blood returning to the heart.

Autoregulation   Self regulation.

Autorhythmic   Capable of spontaneously depolarizing, generating its own rhythm.

Baroreceptors   Arterial pressure receptors that sense changes in blood pressure.

Basophils   A type of granulocyte (white blood cell) that releases histamine and contributes to inflammation.

Bicuspid valve   An alternative name for the left atrioventricular valve.

Blood   The fluid connective tissue that circulates within the blood vessels and heart.

Blood pressure   The force of blood pushing against the walls of blood vessels.

Blood pressure cuff   Apparatus used to measure blood pressure by measuring the amount of air pressure equal to the blood pressure in an artery; also called a sphygmomanometer.

Bohr effect   The reduction in hemoglobin's affinity for oxygen due to decreasing pH or increasing CO_2 levels.

Bradycardia   Abnormally slow heart rate.

Bulk flow   Movement of fluids like air and water from a region of high pressure to a region of low pressure.

Capacitance vessels   Blood vessels, like the veins, that hold a significant portion of the blood volume.

Capillaries   Smallest of the blood vessels, the site of exchange between the tissues and the blood.

Capillary bed   Network of capillaries served by one arteriole.

Capillary exchange   Exchange of oxygen and carbon dioxide in tissue capillaries. Oxygen diffuses from red blood cells to tissue cells; carbon dioxide diffuses in the opposite direction from tissue cells to red blood cells.

Cardiac muscle   Type of muscle tissue found in the heart.

Cardiac output   Volume of blood ejected by each ventricle in one minute; computed by multiplying the heart rate by the stroke volume.

Cardiovascular   Pertaining to the circulatory system.

Cellular respiration   The process in which glucose is broken down to carbon dioxide and water and the energy released is stored in molecules of ATP.

Chemoreceptors   Special cells that detect chemicals.

Circulatory system   Consists of the heart, blood, and blood vessels; delivers nutrients and oxygen to the tissues and carries away wastes.

Clotting factors   Enzymes that trigger the blood-clotting cascade.

Coagulation   The blood-clotting process.

Congestive heart failure   Failure of the heart to pump blood effectively, causing blood to accumulate in the lungs.

Cooperative binding   The principle that the binding of one substrate molecule to a compound increases the ability of that compound to bind more substrate molecules.

Coronary arteries   The arteries that provide oxygen and nutrients to the heart muscle.

Deoxyhemoglobin   Hemoglobin that has no oxygen bound to it.

Desmosomes   Adhesion proteins that tightly bind cardiac muscle fibers together.

Diastole   In the heartbeat cycle, the relaxation phase between contractions; opposite of systole.

Diffusion   Random movement of molecules from a region of higher concentration to one of lower concentration.

Electrocardiogram (ECG or EKG)   Graphic record of heart's action potentials.

Eosinophils   A type of granulocyte (white blood cell) that fights parasitic infections.

Erythrocytes   *See* Red blood cells.

Erythropoietin   Hormone produced in the kidneys that stimulates the production of red blood cells.

Fibrin   Protein strands that stabilize a blood clot.

Filtration   Passage of water and solutes through a membrane as a result of hydrostatic pressure.

Gap junctions   Openings that link the cytoplasm of one cell with that of another; found in cardiac muscle cells.

Globin   Globular protein component of hemoglobin and other molecules.

Globulins   A class of blood plasma proteins; includes antibodies.

Heart attack   Condition that occurs when the blood supply to part of the heart muscle (the myocardium) is reduced or stopped due to blockage of one or more of the coronary arteries; also called myocardial infarction.

Heart rate   The rate at which the heart contracts and relaxes; initiated in the sinoatrial (SA) node of the heart.

Hematocrit   Percent volume of red blood cells in blood.

Hematopoiesis   Production of the formed elements of the blood.

Hematopoietic stem cells   Immature cells found in the bone marrow that give rise to white and red blood cells and platelets.

Heme   Nonprotein, iron-containing component of hemoglobin.

Hemoglobin   Respiratory pigment that binds oxygen; found in red blood cells.

Hemophilia   Group of hereditary blood-clotting disorders.

Hemorrhage   Bleeding.

Inferior vena cava   The major vein returning blood from the lower body regions to the heart.

Intercalated discs   Tight connections between cardiac muscle fibers.

Kwashiorkor   Protein-deficiency disease characterized by swelling of the abdomen.

Leukocytes   *See* White blood cells.

Lymphocytes   Type of leukocyte, or white blood cell, involved in immune function.

Megakaryocytes   Precursor cells that give rise to platelets.

Monocytes   White blood cells that develop into macrophages, engulfing infectious agents.

Myocardial infarction   Medical term for heart attack.

Neutrophils   An abundant type of granulocyte (white blood cell) that fights infection.

Osmosis   The diffusion of water from a region of higher concentration of water (lower concentration of solutes) to a region of lower concentration of water (higher concentration of solutes).

P wave   A deflection wave of an ECG; represents the depolarization of the atria.

Pacemaker cells   Cells of the SA node that are autorhythmic.

Pericardium   The tough covering that protects the heart and anchors it in the chest cavity.

Plaque   Patchlike deposits of fat that form on the walls of blood vessels.

Plasma   The liquid, noncellular portion of the blood.

Platelets   Cell fragments found in the blood and involved in the clotting process.

Polymorphonuclear granulocytes   A class of white blood cells that shows a multilobed nucleus when stained; includes eosinophils, basophils, and neutrophils.

Precapillary sphincters   Circular muscles that control the openings to capillary beds.

Prothrombin   Inactive form of the blood enzyme thrombin.

Pulmonary circuit   The portion of the circulatory system that carries blood between the heart and the lungs.

Pulmonary semilunar valve   Heart valve that separates the right ventricle from the pulmonary trunk, which carries deoxygenated blood to the lungs.

Purkinje fibers   Branching cardiac muscle fibers that originate from the atrioventricular bundle in the atrioventricular (AV) node, extending out to the papillary muscles and lateral walls of the ventricles.

QRS complex   Represents depolarization of the ventricles on an ECG.

Reabsorption   Process by which tissue fluid passes back into the capillaries.

Red blood cells   The cells of the blood that contain the respiratory pigment hemoglobin and deliver oxygen to the body tissues; also known as erythrocytes.

Resistance vessels   Blood vessels that affect blood pressure by increasing or decreasing their diameters.

Respiratory pump   In normal respiration, contractions of the diaphragm that increase the pressure gradient between peripheral veins and vena cavae, thereby promoting the return of venous blood to the heart.

Saturation curve   The graphic representation of the relationship between the oxygen concentration of the environment and the degree of saturation of a molecule like hemoglobin with oxygen.

Serum   Blood plasma without its clotting proteins.

Sinoatrial node   Also known as the SA node, the region within the right atrium of the heart that generates the heart rhythm.

Skeletal muscle pump   "Booster" pump for the heart, promoting venous blood return to the heart through contractions of skeletal muscles.

Stroke volume   Volume of blood pumped out of the ventricles by each heartbeat.

Superior vena cava   The major vein returning blood from the upper body regions to the heart.

Systemic circuit   The portion of the circulatory system that supplies the systemic tissues (all tissues except the lungs).

Systole   The phase of the heartbeat cycle in which the heart muscle contracts.

T wave   A deflection wave of an ECG. Represents repolarization (relaxation) of the ventricles.

Tachycardia   Abnormally rapid heart rate.

Thrombin   Blood enzyme that triggers fibrin formation during the blood-clotting process.

Tricuspid valve   Alternative name for the right atrioventricular valve.

Universal donor blood type   Blood that is O negative—that is, blood containing A, B, and Rh antigens, which can be donated to individuals of any blood type.

Universal recipient blood type   Blood that is AB positive—that is, blood containing A, B, and Rh antigens on the surface of its red blood cells. AB-positive blood can receive transfusions from any other blood type.

Vasoconstrict   Decrease the diameter of a blood vessel.

Vasodilate   Increase the diameter of a blood vessel.

Veins   Muscular blood vessels that carry blood to the heart.

Venous return   Movement of blood back to the heart in the veins.

Ventricles   Chambers of the heart that pump blood into circulation.

Venules   Small veins that collect blood leaving the capillaries.

White blood cells   The cells of the blood that fight infection and disease; also known as leukocytes.

Bibliography

American Heart Association. "Atherosclerosis," Available online. Retrieved June 5, 2008. URL: http://www. americanheart.org/.

American Heart Association. "Ventricular Fibrillation," Available online. Retrieved June 5, 2008. URL: http://www. americanheart.org/.

American Heart Association. "Ventricular Tachycardi," Available online. Retrieved June 5, 2008. URL: http://www. americanheart.org/.

Badylak, S.F. "Regenerative Medicine Approach to Heart Valve Replacement." *Circulation* 111 (2005): 2715–2716.

BBC News. "Heart Valve Grown From Stem Cells," Available online. Retrieved June 5, 2008. URL: http://newsvote.bbc. co.uk/mpapps/pagetools/print/.

Biotechnology and Biological Sciences Research Council. "Scientists Overcome Major Obstacles To Stem Cell Heart Repair," ScienceDaily. Available online. Retrieved June 15, 2008. URL: http://www.sciencedaily.com /releases/2007/1 2/071212201501.htm.

BloodBook.com. "Common Blood Substitutes," Available online. Retrieved June 2, 2008. URL: http://www.bloodbook.com/ substitute.html.

Daily Telegraph. "First Bioartificial Heart May Signal End of Organ Shortage," Available online. Retrieved June 14, 2008. URL: http://telegraph.co.uk/core/Content/.

Transplant News. "Heart Transplant Patient OK After 28 Years," Available online. Retrieved June 14, 2008, from http://www.cbsnews.com/stories/2006/09/14/ap/health/.

"Emergency Rooms to Experiment with Artificial Blood," CNN Interactive. Available online. URL: http://www.cnn. com/HEALTH/9702/17/nfm/ artificial.blood.

Greenemeier, L. "New Blood Substitutes Promise Relief for Sagging Blood Banks," *Scientific American Online.* Available online. Retrieved June 2, 2008. URL: http://www. sciam.com/article/cfm?id+blood-substitutes-hemoglobin-anemia&print=true.

Lewis, R. *Human Genetics: Concepts and Applications.* 3rd ed. New York: WCB McGraw-Hill, 1999.

Marieb, Elaine N. *Human Anatomy and Physiology.* 6th ed. San Francisco: Benjamin Cummings, 2003.

Mayo Clinic. "Statins: Are These Cholesterol-Lowering Drugs Right For You?" Available online. Retrieved June 5, 2008. URL: http://www.mayoclinic.com/.

"New Method To Create An Artificial Heart May Hold Promise For Transplant Surgery," ScienceDaily. Available online. Retrieved June 14, 2008. URL: http://www.science-daily.com /releases/2008/02/080224141414.htm.

"New Recommendations for Blood Pressure." National Heart, Lung, and Blood Institute report. 2003.

"NHLBI Issues New High Blood Pressure Clinical Practice Guidelines," NIH News. Available online. URL: http:// www.nhlbi.nih.gov/new/press/nhlbi-06.htm.

NHBLI Diseases and Conditions Index. "What is an Arrhythmia?" Available online. Retrieved June 5, 2008. URL: http://www.nhlbi.nih.gov/health/dci/Diseases/arr/arr_whatis.html.

NHBLI Diseases and Conditions Index. "What is a Pacemaker?" Available online. Retrieved June 5, 2008. URL: http://www.nhlbi.nih.gov/health/dci/Diseases/pace/pace_all.html.

Saladin, K. *Anatomy and Physiology: The Unity of Form and Function.* 1st ed. New York: WCB McGraw-Hill, 1998.

Shier, D., J. Butler, and R. Lewis. *Hole's Human Anatomy and Physiology.* 8th ed. New York: WCB McGraw-Hill, 1999.

Society of Thoracic Surgeons. "Mitral Valve Replacement." Available online. Retrieved June 5, 2008. URL: http://

www.sts.org/sections/patientinformation/valvesurgery/
mitralvalvereplacement/.

University of Michigan Health System. "Could Heart Transplants Become A Thing Of The Past?" ScienceDaily. Available online. Retrieved June 15, 2008. URL: http://www.
sciencedaily.com/releases/2008/06/080602231622.htm.

Vander, A., J. Sherman, and D. Luciano. *Human Physiology:
The Mechanism of Body Function.* 8th ed. New York:
McGraw-Hill, 2001.

Further Resources

Web Sites

American Heart Association
www.americanheart.org
Information about atherosclerosis and heart attack

American Red Cross
www.redcross.org

Ames Center for Gravitational Biology Research, NASA
http://cgbr.arc.nasa.gov

National Heart, Lung, and Blood Institute
www.nhlbi.nih.gov

National Women's Health Information Center
www.4women.gov

Vanderbilt Center for Space Physiology and Medicine
www.mc.vanderbilt.edu/gcrc/space/

Picture Credits

Page

12: © Infobase Publishing
16: © Infobase Publishing
20: © Infobase Publishing
22: © Infobase Publishing
24: © Infobase Publishing
27: © Infobase Publishing
35: © Infobase Publishing
37: © Infobase Publishing
39: © Infobase Publishing
43: Dr. Stanley Flegler/
Visuals Unlimited, Inc.
44: © Infobase Publishing
48: © Infobase Publishing
49: © Infobase Publishing
50: Dr. Fred Hossler/Visuals
Unlimited, Inc./Infobase
Publishing

52: © Infobase Publishing
58: © Infobase Publishing
61: © Infobase Publishing
65: © Infobase Publishing
67: © Infobase Publishing
68: © Infobase Publishing
71: © Infobase Publishing
87: © Infobase Publishing
89: © Infobase Publishing
93: © Infobase Publishing
95: © Infobase Publishing
97: © Infobase Publishing
99: © Infobase Publishing
100: © Infobase Publishing

Index

About the Author

Dr. Susan Whittemore, Ph.D., is a professor of biology at Keene State College in Keene, New Hamphsire. She received a master's degree from Utah State University and her Ph.D. in physiology from Dartmouth Medical School in 1991. She also completed a postdoctoral program in molecular endocrinology at Dartmouth before arriving at Keene State in 1993. Dr. Whittemore teaches a wide range of biology courses for nonmajors, including Exploring Genes, A Brave New World (a writing course on the ethics of biotechnology), Forensic Science, and Human Anatomy and Physiology. In addition, she teaches an introductory biology course, Cells and Physiology, Comparative Animal Physiology, Ecophysiology, and Endocrine Disruption. She was a recipient of a National Science Foundation grant supporting her work in molecular physiology. She was a contributing author to Scott Freeman's *Biological Sciences* (2002), an introductory biology text published by Prentice Hall.

קודש